Dancing through the darkness

A troubled Soul's adventures to find the answers she needed to heal.

Cristina Pav

Copyright © 2024 Cristina Pavlidis

ISBN
Print: 978-1-923216-04-4

This work is copyright. Apart from any use permitted under the *Copyright Act 1968*, no part of this publication may be reproduced, stored in a retrieval system or transmitted in any form or by any means, electronic, mechanical, photocopying, recording or otherwise, without the prior written permission of Cristina Pavlidis.

The information in this book is based on the author's experiences and opinions. The author and publisher disclaim responsibility for any adverse consequences, which may result from use of the information contained herein. Permission to use any external content has been sought by the author. Any breaches will be rectified in further editions of the book.

Cover design: Busybird Publishing

Layout and typesetting: Busybird Publishing

Busybird Publishing
2/118 Para Road
Montmorency, Victoria
Australia 3094
www.busybird.com.au

Contents

Introduction	i
1. Early Years	1
2. Teenage Years	8
3. First Spiritual Encounter	13
4. Drugs and Band Scene	20
5. Kelly	25
6. Spreading My Wings	28
7. Sydney Nightlife and Encounters	37
8. Back in Melbourne	47
9. Warning Signs	49
10. London	57
11. Memorable London Dates	61
12. Mayfair and Soho Clubs	67
13. Bahrain – The Pearl in the Gulf	72
14. London Oil Sheikhs	81
15. Back to Bahrain	87
16. Back in London	91
17. Back Home	101
18. Martial Arts and Buddhism	110
19. Six Weeks of Bliss – Enlightenment	116
20. Dance and Movement Training	120
21. Swami	124
22. Mary from Bahrain	127
23. Relationship	135
24. Holiday with Symptoms	142

25. Home and Cancer Scare	161
26. Dance Therapy Classes – The Answer!	167
27. Dakini Dance – My Performance	170
28. Leo in Barcelona	174
29. COVID and Beyond	181
Acknowledgements and Reflections	187

Introduction

We all have stories to tell and this is mine. The journey of my life was filled with dance, spiritual experiences, and encounters with some powerful and high-profile people during my travels – many of whom were well-known in the music industry and the arts.

I was always a creative person and dancing is where I felt at home. For many reasons (including my background coming from a migrant family), there was no pathway or support for me to pursue my dream. As a girl, all I saw in front of me was a life where I was told I was only good for working in an office. There was no scope for getting a dancing career and living the life I wanted. I was lost and looking to fill the void within me. The adventures I had, although unconventional, allowed me to embrace my love of dance and express myself freely.

I dedicate this to all the people in search of answers to life's unexpected challenges and the lessons from them. Everything I attracted in my life helped me to become my own greatest teacher. Whether it was positive or negative, it all contributed to my growth. It took me a long time to really understand this concept on a Soul level... I had read many books on spiritual growth, however, I needed lived experience to fully understand it.

Despite how much I believed in it, doubt did rear its ugly head many times to distract me – to take me off track. I went through the darkness until I finally pulled myself out of it. Through the help of the energy I call Source, I started healing myself by reaching to the light within... to accept who I am, open my heart once again and believe in the real me!

I know now this is the path my Soul has chosen for me, to help me get back into the natural state of flow and allow synchronicity to flow back into my life again. I feel I'm now back on track and my growth has expanded three-fold, especially facing my biggest challenges – getting past a couple of major crises.

I chose to be here, so I fought all the challenges presented until my answers emerged from my personal battles to be at peace. It's possible to find your own happiness again once your heart opens up. This is how I choose to live – to be more present and aware.

1

Early Years

My parents, John and Maria, had immigrated to Australia from Greece by boat soon after they married. They decided to start a new life here, as there were many opportunities offered to immigrants by the Australian government. They boarded the ship on a month-long journey with my two sisters, Freda and Goula. I was born the following year. Later on my two brothers, George and Michael, were born. The first brother arrived when I was eight years old. I was the youngest of the three sisters and we were only one year apart. Michael came much later.

I was born at the Royal Women's Hospital in Carlton. My mum said this was thanks to a street sweeper who, in the early hours of the morning, helped her get to hospital in time by flagging down a car that I was almost born in.

I grew up in Fitzroy, a small suburb of Melbourne, close to the city centre. It was a fantastic area, and still is a popular inner-city location. The parks, transport and shops were all walking distance from where we lived, and the city was only a short tram ride away. The main shopping area near our place was Smith Street and there was always a buzz in the air, always something happening.

Fitzroy was a thriving place to live – a close-knit community. There were lots of Greek immigrants living there, and many Italians too. My father worked long hours for a big meat distribution company in the city. He was a hard worker and saved for a deposit to buy his own house. Later, he paid a deposit on a shop in Brunswick Street and opened a butcher shop. I remember going there to help out reluctantly. I wasn't happy helping with the cleaning of meat. It wasn't my idea of fun. Eventually my father gave up on me helping out, as I always avoided going there and when I did, I cringed at the meat he was cutting up and the blood spots I got on my cleaning rag.

During the time Dad and Mum worked together in their butcher shop, my sister Goula and I would head out exploring to see what was happening around the area. We loved that we could get out while our parents weren't home. Our eldest sister Freda always refused to join us. She was more interested in dress-up, so we would set off together happily, open to any adventures we could find during those few available hours we could sneak out of the house.

One afternoon on our adventures, we noticed there was a banquet held for the Plastic Surgeons' Association at the nearby gardens, so we both strolled into the marquee set up for the event. We were young girls of about eight and nine years of age and on entering we looked up at the men in their dark suits, who looked very distinguished drinking wine and chatting in their groups. We noticed there were lots of fancy foods spread out on crisp, white tablecloths. The temptation was too much, so we helped ourselves to an assortment of unusual tastings. There were mainly finger foods and they were so delicious. After a few minutes helping ourselves to these new delights, a middle-aged gentleman asked us, "Who are you with?"

At that I blurted out, "My dad!" And pointed to a stranger nearby. My sister and I both looked at each other and knew that it was time to exit before we got found out. In an instant, we sprinted out of the marquee, giggling and happy that we got away. Together, we walked through the gardens to get home before Mum returned from the shop.

On hot days, when we needed to cool off, we would sometimes go swimming in the pond at the Exhibition Gardens where the yabbies were in abundance. The water was dirty, and we weren't aware of the possible consequences. We would bring a bucket or a jar with us and look for yabbies to take home, and then jump in for a swim. When we got home, Mum would be horrified to see us wet and dirty. We were sent to the bathroom immediately to wash and change our clothes.

Mum was always wondering what mischief we were up to when she noticed us missing after a quick trip to the shops to get groceries. When we got back home she would throw her hands in the air to show how upset she was with us for leaving the house. She always instructed us to stay with our older sister – who was too busy grooming herself to notice us leave most of the time.

There were days we wanted to buy an ice cream or drink from the local shop, so we devised ways of getting the three pennies or sixpence we needed to buy our treats. On a couple of occasions, we tried knocking on doors and when the owner of the house would open the door, I would do the talking. I told them we had a raffle going to win a purse and it only cost a penny each. I used to bring along a Glomesh purse I owned that was given to me by my next-door neighbour to show them what the prize was. We would buy the raffle tickets from our local shop and give them out in exchange for the small amount we received. We soon had enough to use for our treats. I'm sure they knew we just wanted it for an ice cream! Usually we would only knock on doors until we got enough for our treats, then we would head off home licking our ice creams happily! Eventually, Mum found out from one of the neighbours and said she would tell Dad if we did it again, so that soon stopped.

I already had an idea of what I loved to do with a passion, and that was to dance. The live pop show would come on TV with all their dancers, and I would imitate them as best as I could. When I didn't know the words to a song, I sang and made up my own. I would spend hours composing my own dance steps after I had watched the performers on the television. I couldn't remember all the steps but I was always able to feel the music surge through me. As a result I would start improvising and it usually turned out great!

I also loved acting and my favourite role would be playing dead – you should have seen the face on my older sister when I first played that prank on her. Her face went white until I opened my eyes and smiled back at her. She chased me around the house until we were both exhausted.

One clear memory of my early years was waiting for my grandfather, Tony, to come to visit my mum. He was a tall man with strong features and he was fit – he usually walked from his home in Northcote to our place in Fitzroy. What I remember about him was that he was very generous and went out a lot. He was usually out when I went to visit my grandmother. She would always make me a cup of tea and crusty toast when I went to her home. I loved dipping the bread into the tea – so yummy!

Sometimes my father would yell at me and that made me very upset. It often happened when I answered him back in frustration, because he was always ordering me around. I thought he was quite demanding – after all, I was only a young girl then. There was one time he was coming down the stairs from his bedroom, then asked me to go up and get something for him. I told him to get it himself. He responded by running after me. I didn't want him to catch me, as I knew what his temper was like. I ran to the front door and took off immediately to my grandmother's house in Northcote. I walked all the way, which took me well over an hour, thinking about why I wouldn't go back home.

This happened more than once. When I arrived, Baba would greet me, feed me some treats, and let me stay the night. I would go home the next day when I was reassured that Dad wouldn't punish me. I remember she never scolded me for leaving my father's house, and I felt that she was a saint for being there for me during those times.

When my grandfather visited he would bring along a handful of pennies, stack them on the ground and ask me to dance for him, which I willingly did! I danced to my heart's delight, and as a bonus, I got paid! I so looked forward to his visits as I knew he always brought us sweets, too. Dancing was where I felt I belonged, and I was good at it. This is where my focus remained from an early age. It still is something I love with a passion.

A relative of mine – who lived interstate – was in a well-known band that was very popular during the 60s, playing gigs in Sydney. He came to visit us at home in Melbourne one day and saw me dancing. He commented a few years later that he recognised I had a talent and said he had expressed that to my dad. But Dad wouldn't allow him to take me interstate to be groomed for a dancing career. I was only ten years old then, and my father wouldn't agree to let me leave home at such a young age.

Every time he visited Melbourne he would come to visit us, especially Mum (as he was her close relative), and if I was around I would dance. He liked my enthusiasm and love for dance. I would freely dance for anyone if they asked me, and everyone could see how passionate I was.

This was a memory I always held on to, as it was the most positive comment I had ever received at that young age. The fact that it was coming from an established musician gave me the confirmation I needed to know I was good at dancing, and so I wanted to dance even more.

My primary school years were at George Street State School – it was very close to our home. Mum walked me there and I remember how proud I was of her and how beautiful and caring she was.

My earliest memory of attending primary school was that it was fairly strict. There were two teachers in particular that were imprinted in my mind.

In grade one we had Miss Miller, who was a stern, older teacher of average height and slim build. Her manner terrified me. She was very abrupt and when she spoke even the boys didn't dare talk back. I was too afraid to ask if I could use the girls' toilet during class one day, and I ended up wetting my pants. I was so embarrassed – I had created a puddle on the floor. I stayed on that spot until the teacher saw it and contacted my Mum to come and take me home to change my clothes. At lunch time I went home with Mum, visibly upset. I remember I wore red overalls that day.

The other teacher was Mr Harris, my grade three teacher. He was talking to us but I wasn't paying full attention to him. I was sitting in the back row and asked someone next to me about what the teacher was saying. The next minute he came storming over to me, grabbed me by my hair and dragged me to the front of the class. I was crying as he was hurting me. He made me sit at the front for the remainder of the class.

I found school to be too controlling and structured. I didn't enjoy my early years there. I already knew I was a free spirit and disliked school as it was so disciplined. Where was the fun and laughter? I couldn't wait to get home and play outside with my neighbours and have fun on the weekends with my sister.

I remember being interested in God at a young age. Once, some people in my neighbourhood with strong religious beliefs were talking about the end of the world in the year 2000. I told my friend Sophie, "It's okay, Jesus loves me and he will save me."

I was only about seven years old when those words came out of my mouth. My family hardly ever went to church except for celebrations and invitations, so it was a surprise to hear myself say that. I was already curious about the meaning of life at an early age.

2

Teenage Years

By the end of primary school I had become more or less a wallflower. You would hardly have noticed me. I always sat at the back of the classroom as quiet as a mouse, hoping not to get noticed – I wasn't very confident with myself back then. I was also the tallest during those early years in class and felt somewhat awkward in my own skin.

It was only when I attended a girls' school in Fitzroy that my growth spurt slowed down and I felt happier in my body. Mum had taken me to the doctor after she became worried about my sudden growth spurt. I had grown almost a foot taller in 10 months. The doctor prescribed some hormone tablets for a short time, to control it.

I won a scholarship in my second year at high school, so my parents didn't have to pay any more tuition for me. I was quite a bright girl and had a good memory, so I got good grades even if I only studied the night before a test.

I started gradually mixing with the other girls at my new school. Before then, I hadn't mixed with others much. My sisters were at the same school so I would follow them around whenever I was bored.

There was a group of three Italian girls in my class that were interested in the guys who were living across the street, in a double-storey brick home almost opposite the school. They were determined to meet them, so they came up with many ideas until they all agreed on one plan. They dared me to go across the street during lunch time and knock on the door, pretending I was doing a survey. I wanted to be a part of their group so I felt I had to do it. I took a clipboard and paper and pen and hesitantly walked up to the house, with the girls giggling away behind me. I knocked and a beautiful, slim blonde lady dressed in soft, flowing clothes answered. I noticed she had a beautiful soft aura, and she smiled and invited me inside.

I was in awe of what I saw once I entered the house. There were so many interesting types of people living there. I found out there were budding actors and teachers and university students – it was a busy household.

One of the people living there was Red Symons, who was a school teacher at the time. He was pleasant to me when Jenny introduced us, but not interested in taking the survey. Jenny – who was his girlfriend then – was so friendly; she offered me a cup of tea and asked me about myself. I was comfortable chatting to her and after some time I got up to leave, thanking her for allowing me into her home. To my surprise, she told me to drop in whenever I liked. It was an offer I couldn't refuse – I wanted to be in that scene, so I accepted!

Whenever I could, I went to visit Jenny and take my sister Goula with me. The three Italian school friends had to go home straight after school, so they couldn't come with me. They weren't really confident enough to meet my new friends – it had just been a dare. I was always so happy that I had been brave enough to go and knock on the door! It was so fun to be there – surrounded by actors and musicians dropping in to visit. There was always an acoustic guitar being played somewhere in the house.

Soon after, Red started rehearsing in a warehouse down the same street with his newly formed band Skyhooks. I heard one of his first gigs was held at my school, but I didn't go, as I found out too late. They also had a singer called Steve. When he left the band afterwards, they took on a new singer called 'Shirley', and that's when they became very successful. His voice was so unique – exactly what the band needed! I didn't see them at their peak as I was overseas by that time.

Around that time, I also started visiting the warehouse where the rehearsals were held. I had met the owners at Jenny's house one time and was invited to drop in whenever I wanted. Eventually that became my choice of place to visit after school. A lot of musicians were dropping in there and jamming. It became more comfortable for me to be around that scene than at the house, as it was also a much larger space. I felt very welcomed there. I was always meeting someone new – there was never a dull moment.

I noticed a guy working at Jenny's house on the roof one day. He was hammering away. Eventually, after a few days, I paused to have a proper good look at him just when the guy decided to look down at me. We smiled, caught in the act of checking each other out – it was good timing. I quite liked how he presented. He was much older than I was – in his mid-twenties compared to my youthful fifteen – and on hearing him speak I noticed he had an English accent. He told me his name was James. He asked me to wait, then came down to formally introduce himself.

The first thing I noticed was how cool he looked, with hair to his shoulders that he tied back when he worked. He was missing part of a finger, and explained how it happened in an accident at a job years ago. He told me he was a carpenter and explained how he would be working on the roof for a while repairing it. I was very shy, but besotted by him. I didn't talk to him long that day, but every day from then on I spoke to him briefly during my lunch break or after school. This went on for a few weeks. I couldn't wait to see him, as he was a very happy person and so attentive towards me.

About a month later, he was taking a break in the house. We had quite a rapport by now, he beckoned me to come into the living area. That was when I allowed him to kiss me for the first time. I felt such a stirring within me – it was the longest kiss ever! Whenever we saw each other after that, we always just kissed and cuddled. He was quite a gentleman and never pressed for more.

I remember one day he invited me to his home in North Carlton and it was there I met his girlfriend. She introduced herself and I was surprised to hear that she was the daughter of the owner of one of the biggest department stores in Australia.

She was very pleasant and told me many stories, including ones about her brother who was then travelling through India. She kept me interested with the tales of many travel adventures. I could see she was very wise – she had a lot of knowledge about life and was very articulate with her choice of words. I sensed she was very comfortable in her skin, and although average in looks, was beautiful as a person. Her energy was soft and her dark clothes worn loose, maybe because she was a little overweight then. She was sitting on a rocking chair and I even recall she had knitting close by.

I hadn't known that James was in a relationship, and immediately after meeting his girlfriend I lost interest in him. I didn't want to see him again. I guess this was how he wanted me to find out about his relationship – without telling me. I really liked his partner, so I understood how he would care for her. I know he was fond of me and had to let me go.

He was the first guy I kissed. I knew it was just the beginning and there would be more adventures to come.

3

First Spiritual Encounter

One afternoon after school on a pleasant day, I walked past a terrace house with a few men sitting on armchairs on the front porch. One of them smiled at me and then, to get my attention, commented on how he liked girls in school uniform. I instantly recognised him as the drummer from a well-known band the La De Da's. I loved their latest song, "Gonna See My Baby Tonight", and was humming it to myself day and night. I also recognised the other band members from seeing them on TV.

It was such a surprise to see them so close to my home. There was Kevin Borich, Ronnie Peel, Phil Key, and the owner of the house who I later found out was called Danny Robinson. I was a young fifteen-year-old in awe of them. Keith, the drummer, again mentioned he liked girls in school uniform and I blushed. I decided to keep on walking, as I didn't have the courage to talk to them on my own.

I told my girlfriend Kerrie about them at school. The next day we were both hanging out the front of the house after school finished, hoping we could see the band mem-bers. The lady of the house came out and introduced herself. She told us that they left that morning and then asked us about ourselves. I then told her I lived in a white-painted double-storey bluestone house two blocks down. That's when her eyes lit up and she asked me if I wanted to babysit her daughter, Amy, as she needed help at times. I told her I was only too happy to help – especially if I could hang out close to the band members. I soon found out that the band only stayed there when they were in Melbourne, but that didn't matter. I would keep going over to babysit Amy and eventually they would be back to perform again.

Kerrie went home as soon as she heard the band had left, but was eager for me to let her know when they were back in town. She was my best friend at the time. She had a very voluptuous figure, was big breasted and wore her tunic dress up high to her buttocks. Whenever she bent over, her panties were intentionally on display. I started wearing my tunic slightly above my knee when I began hanging out with her.

Just across the road from the house was the Siddha Yoga Ashram. I was walking past it one afternoon when a middle-aged man wearing an orange beanie called out to me from his seat. He was sitting on a bench in the garden area when he saw me and beckoned me to come inside. I smiled back but decided to keep walking that first time.

The next day I went to meet Amy after school, but on the way I also decided to walk past the front of the Yoga Ashram, as I was curious. I was interested in knowing more about this new centre and what it was all about. There was something that drew me to the place so, seeing as it was on the way, I decided to have another look.

The same man I'd seen previously was outside again, and he smiled at me. I paused and he quickly walked to the front gate of the centre. He then reached over and patted my head. I felt a surge of energy rush up that took me by surprise. My first thought was, *Who is this older man?* I knew deep down he was someone unique, as I felt drawn to his energy on our first encounter. I felt a charge running through my spine and my head was alight. I didn't know what he did, but I got a little scared and walked off without a word. My chakras were clearly opening up my energy centres. I didn't understand what was going on at that moment, until I learnt more about Kundalini and the chakras' relationship to the body at a later stage. I also remember thinking there was something sexual about that man.

Years later, I dated a man who went to the same centre. I heard a talk there one day about the famous Guru Muktananda, who had passed away some years after I met him during his visit to Melbourne. The speaker was talking about how meeting such an esteemed, enlightened being would be better than winning the lottery. My first thoughts were, *Why didn't I win the lottery?*

At this lecture they also spoke about Gurumayi, who was the Muktananda's successor, and then we were led into a meditation. We were instructed to close our eyes and Gurumayi was to appear in our guided meditation. This is what I saw.

She was with me and we were running through a lush garden as young girls, aged around five or six. It was a very serene and beautiful, vivid setting, with green grass and trees around us. We were being playful and happy, with nature surrounding us. Our energies were radiant as we ran along together, holding hands like best friends.

When it was time to talk about what vision came up for the group, everyone who participated in the meditation was asked to share. I didn't dare tell the group that I saw Gurumayi as my equal. I decided to keep quiet and listen to the stories, which were mainly of people revering her and putting her on a pedestal. I was amused at some of the stories being told – I was imagining their reaction at me telling them my story.

I didn't realise that meeting Muktananda was going to set me onto a path of looking within, but it was the beginning of my spiritual quest, which has remained with me from that day on.

I continued visiting Amy at the house where the La De Da's stayed, and it was there I met her cousin, Linda, when she was staying there during a visit from interstate. She was very friendly and about four years older than I was. She had experienced much more than I had. I was drawn to her maturity, so I ended up visiting her often to catch up on any gossip. She was a lot more interesting than any of my other friends.

One day, Linda mentioned she was going to go to the country for a break and said that if I wanted, I could come along. I had just turned sixteen and was aching for some adventure. I asked my mother; she wouldn't allow me to go. But I was determined to go, and the rebel in me was already apparent. I soon packed my bag and left with my newest friend Linda. We arrived after four hours driving through the countryside in her car. I was excited to see where she was taking me. When we finally arrived, I saw that Linda had booked us into a caravan park – it was my first time staying in a caravan. I didn't know what to expect there; however, to my surprise on that same day, a group of three Canadian men arrived, checked in and stayed in one of the caravans opposite us.

One of them, whose name was Michael, I fancied in particular. I saw he liked me as well as he immediately introduced himself wearing a big smile. We soon got chatting. He always had his guitar with him, ready to serenade me with his beautiful music whenever he saw me. He told me he was a musician travelling through Australia with his friends. He had long black hair, a gentle spoken man in his twenties. I loved to sit and listen to him play his guitar.

First Spiritual Encounter

One night, after a few days, it turned extremely cold and the wind was howling. As usual, my girlfriend Linda was out visiting others in the neighbouring caravans. She would usually stay out all night. I was listening to the wind and feeling cold, only with a thin makeshift blanket, when I heard a knock on the door. I opened it to see Michael carrying a sleeping bag. He asked me if he could stay the night and sleep next to me. He said we could share each other's bedding and be extra warm. I happily agreed to his offer. I didn't expect anything to happen between us, however I was happy that he wanted to be close to me and keep me warm. It turned out to be the night that I gave myself to a man for the first time. It was a gentle experience, one I never have forgotten. It was filled with so much passion, we had such a great connection, it was electric!

In the morning, he gradually made his way back to his friends and he said we would see each other later. He also told me they were leaving later in the afternoon and although I was sad to see him go, I wasn't emotional about it. Before he left the caravan I gave him a memento of our night together, a ring made of silver with a couple united on it. It was made by a famous jeweller who I had met through my sister Goula – she knew lots of artists from Carlton. He had liked me, so after we visited him a few times at his place, he had given me one of his rings as a gift. I told Michael to keep it in memory of our night together, and he accepted it graciously. We spent the afternoon together enjoying the sun and listening to sweet music until he was ready to leave – he was to continue on his travels through Australia. His friends were teasing him when he came to kiss me for the last time.

Early that evening when I was going back to my caravan, I bumped into a man I hadn't met before. He looked like he was in his early forties and was staying next door to me. He asked me without hesitation if I was interested in being in a blue movie – I would make lots of money, and to think about it and let him know by tomorrow.

I went to bed thinking about it, not knowing what a blue movie was. I thought maybe it's coloured blue, it's some alternative type of movie. I was in bed thinking about taking his offer, after all I was going to get a job and be in a movie too! Deciding to speak to him about it the next day, I laid my head down to sleep. Only a few hours had passed when I heard a loud knocking on my door. It was the police.

I was surprised to see them. They said they were looking for Linda, and I told them she wasn't with me, so they started knocking on the other caravan doors and found her with some guy drinking. They soon arrested us both and took us away. They placed me in a cell that night alone as it was too late to take me somewhere else to stay. It was a frightening experience, a real jail!

The next morning a female officer brought me a decent breakfast – an omelette, toast and juice – and then questioned me about my friend. I found out that the owners of the caravan park had made a complaint about my friend, she was hopping from caravan to caravan every night and drinking with the men and they had made a complaint. They wanted to charge her for kidnapping me as well because my parents had reported me missing. I was told that if she was twenty-one she would have been in serious trouble, because I had only just turned sixteen.

After they finished questioning me, they drove me to a girl's remand centre and placed me there. I didn't know how long I would be held. I had to wear a grey tunic with a white T-shirt top under it and do chores every day, it was so disciplined: you had to be up at a certain time early in the morning, eat at scheduled times, everything was planned! The other girls were teasing me, telling me I would be there for a long time. It was absolutely horrible!

After a few days I was called to see the female warden and when I went to the office my Father and Uncle were there waiting for me. They had come to collect me and take me home. I was so happy! I was afraid of my Dad when he had a temper, but he was fine as long as his brother was with him. I knew he wouldn't raise his voice until I got home. On arrival at home, I was greeted by a much-relieved Mum and I went straight to my bedroom to hide from Dad. I stayed in my room until my Mum came and told me it was okay to come out. Dad had gone out.

I behaved myself after that and was told I wasn't allowed to go and visit the house anymore, I didn't know what happened to Linda after that, I never saw her again.

I realised later that if the police hadn't turned up that night I would have accepted the offer to do a blue movie. Who knows what would have happened to me in that industry?

4

Drugs and Band Scene

It was the early seventies and clubs were springing up everywhere at the same time. I was sixteen, living in Fitzroy close to town, meaning I never had far to travel. There was so much talent out there to be discovered and these venues had brilliant artists and bands playing there that later became icons of their times. I just had to be a part of the scene, and was very eager and now ready to do some dancing out at the clubs.

Dad was always busy with work and I knew that once he came home it would be late in the evening, so he wouldn't miss me as he would go straight to bed. Knowing that he was a sound sleeper, I was safe. I climbed out of my window very quietly, then took the tram close to the city. The place was just on the fringe of Carlton. I had gone alone, and that didn't concern me. Once I started dancing, I knew I owned the floor.

At the club, I met a French pianist called Francois playing for the band. He came over to me during his break, and was very friendly towards me and invited me to party on with him. That night he introduced me to Mandrax tablets, which were popular to take in those days. It was a Barbiturate that was used as a sleeping tablet: once you fought the sleep effects of it, you got a high from it.

I suppose I just wanted to fit in and for him to like me, so I obligingly took one. The effects came on slowly and I was soon feeling very relaxed from it. I felt like I was in a dream state; everything felt soothing and I lost all my inhibitions completely. I wasn't shy anymore.

I became his girlfriend after our first meeting and we soon partied hard together, drinking, smoking pot and popping pills, which all contributed to me shedding all my inhibitions. Besides that, the drugs helped me become more expressive on the dance floor. I was being as creative and unique as I could be. I was, in fact, expressing my inner dance – in those days no one was dancing like me – although shortly after that a new talent emerged. Her name was Kate Bush, and her dancing was very similar to mine.

I went to a place called Bertie's one night after I broke up with Francois. We were only together a short time, maybe two months – it was never anything serious with him. Bertie's was a club located in Spring Street. I also went to Sebastian's near the corner of Victoria Street quite a lot. Another venue was called Much More Ballroom, located in Brunswick Street towards the city end. There were lots of great clubs and I went wherever I heard that there was a good band playing.

I remember Daddy Cool playing there one night, and the guitarist Ross Hannaford jumped off the stage during their break and approached me to ask if I would want to teach him how to move. He had been watching me dance and liked how I improvised to the song 'Eagle Rock'. I started seeing him for a short time after that, casually. He lived near me at that time and I used to bump into him at a local Italian cake shop. He was there for the short black coffees. He was always soft spoken and very polite with me.

I got invited to many parties at the clubs and I met many people, mainly band members, roadies, and their girlfriends. It was a happening scene and people always commented on my dancing style – it made people happy! I remember going to Countdown and having a dance there whenever I could. One day, Meldrum approached me and said he had some ideas for me. However, nothing eventuated, and I didn't bother chasing it up as I was too busy partying and dating. I didn't hold a boyfriend for long though. I guess popping pills didn't help me have a stable relationship, and anyway I was looking for something more.

I was soon a part of the scene due to my unique style of dancing. I was barely seventeen when one night after clubbing, I was on my way out when a guy came up to me and said that he knew my father. I remember he was of Greek origin and I believed him when he mentioned my father … after all he knew his name. He convinced me to get a lift home with him. I went to his car and saw there were three other men in it. I paused suddenly when I saw them in the car, and immediately the guy named Harry said firmly, "It's okay I know your father," so I decided to take a chance and trust him. I wasn't listening to my gut then as I clearly had been drinking too much on the night. Harry was a clean cut guy and was wearing a thick gold chain that looked a bit ostentatious, tall and very fit looking, big biceps, about twenty-three years old. He seemed nice enough, although a bit too pushy in manner.

I was very intoxicated and not aware of where he was driving at first, then I did sense something was not right, it was taking a bit too long to get home. I then saw he was heading into Studley Park Road leading towards the park there. I started to insist that he was going the wrong way, that's when he raised his voice and told me to keep my mouth shut. I knew then, I was going to be raped by all four of these men, I couldn't do a thing about it.

I started to weep openly and they were talking to each other in Greek amongst each other ignoring my pleas. The car went in the park and drove into an area of bushes and distanced from the track. I was thinking to myself now, after they rape me, will they then kill me? I was looking for a miracle. It was after three in the morning, no cars around on the road and Harry had just stopped when out of nowhere a flashlight was directed at us. A police car was patrolling the area and must have seen Harry's car and followed us in.

Two policemen came over to the driver's side to speak to the men. It was a surprise from heaven for me, I was in already in shock and I could see the men became quiet as mice now. I looked at Harry, he looked like he had seen a ghost and he was so scared as to what I was going to say to the police. The policeman came over to me and asked if I was all right and I responded, all the while with Harry looking at me with pleading eyes and mouth open, he was so scared. I answered, "Yes Officer, he is my friend." Then he asked me if I was sure and I said, "Yes." I didn't know what to do, as this could have escalated into something dangerous. These men in the car were not boys and very strong looking. I didn't want any trouble. I'm sure the police took the car details and his license information so if anything happened to me after they left, they would know who they were.

Once the police left, Harry looked at me with a big smile, his friends were also very grateful that I didn't give them up. After many sighs of relief, Harry said, "I'm taking you home right now," and drove me straight to my door on my directions. He also thanked me for not telling the police that I just met him and that he had taken me there instead of home. That night in bed, I thanked God for looking after me. I wanted to forget that close encounter.

Taking Barbiturates on a regular basis helped fill that void temporarily … after all, they do sedate you and numb you from feeling. This didn't stop me from going out dancing after the incident. I just decided I wouldn't take a lift late at night from any man in the future unless I did know them.

5

Kelly

At Sebastian's club one night, I met a lovely girl called Kelly who enjoyed partying like me. I was outside getting some fresh air when Kelly approached me and struck up a conversation. We soon clicked, and chatted openly. We had lots in common so became friends after that night. She was tall and small framed, very thin, and she had lovely long, deep-coloured red hair full of curls. She looked like a doll. We would both would meet up outside the club most weekends and pop a pill or two, and have a drink from a silver flask that Kelly had brought along that was filled with bourbon to drink before we went inside.

It was a fantastic club, there was always room for me to move on the dance floor, and in those days men always bought you drinks and everyone I met appreciated my creative dance style – of course being young and attractive helped too. Kelly didn't really dance much, she would just prop herself against a support like a wall or post to get her balance once she was a bit tipsy and watch me. Whenever she got really excited about the music being played she would have a little boogie with me for a song or two.

I sometimes went to Kelly's house before we went out and I remember at times waiting for up to three hours before she was ready to go. It involved putting her make up on, doing her hair, having a drink in between and finally getting dressed. I was so patient waiting for her to dress at first, but then it was such a drag. Eventually I just told her to meet me there. It only took me fifteen minutes max to get ready and out the door. I didn't wear makeup, couldn't see the point of wearing it. I already could see how the skin couldn't breathe properly with all the packed-on make up. I didn't think it suited me either – I looked good without it.

 I was out one night with Kelly and we went to see a solo performer with his back up band at a local club. I was quite attracted to him, he had mesmerising dark eyes and was originally from London. I had heard he had been a leading man in a few musicals so had to see him for myself. My aunt used to say we were similar in looks, so I was curiously drawn to him and also because he was a great entertainer. Kelly and I were both, as usual, off our faces during his show and we went up close to him in front of the stage. I was directly facing him and got his attention once his show started. I was showing off my dance moves on the dance floor, that's when he noticed me. Once the show ended he came up to me and asked if I wanted to go to his hotel room to party on, I agreed, but I had to bring Kelly along and he said he was okay with that. I thought nothing would happen, seeing it was the two of us together. I was thinking maybe it could turn into a close friendship and date, once he got to know me better that night after a few drinks. How wrong I was to think that!

 We all drank a bit too much in his hotel room and somehow I ended up in bed with him. Kelly climbed into bed after and then I saw them cuddling, I was so tired and fell asleep whilst this was happening. In the morning she told me that they had slept together whilst I was sound asleep. I wasn't expecting that to happen and I was a bit disappointed, I thought he favoured me, but it seemed like he wanted us both! This was just a one-nighter, as I didn't see him again after that.

I saw Kelly quite a lot in that year; she was my closest friend outside of my family, however I was spreading my wings and wanted to start trying out new places. Kelly only frequented the usual clubs closer to the city so as time passed we saw less of each other, as I wanted to explore more.

6

Spreading My Wings

Promoters drove me to gigs so I could dance on stage, but I didn't get paid because I never thought of asking for money. I just wanted to dance and was quite shy, so they took advantage. John Finch, a promoter, used to come and drive me to Frankston where he booked a hall for bands. It felt like miles away. I was offered a few free drinks at the bar before I went on stage, but that was all.

I started dancing at the famous Q Club soon after that. I had met the owner, John Abbott, earlier when he ran his business from his home in South Melbourne – he hired out equipment to bands. I used to pop in to visit him and his partner on a regular basis. So when he opened up the Q Club, I already had my foot in the door. He always had the top headliners playing, which made it a popular venue.

One night, one of the biggest bands of the 70s, Sherbet, was playing. I was dancing on one side of the stage and the audience threw coins at me – they were impressed by my dancing. I just picked up the coins and continued dancing. I gained some new fans that night.

After the show, Garth, the keyboard player, asked me to join them, so I got into their limousine. All the fans banged on the window, asking me how I got invited. I went with them to their hotel, and the rest of the night was more or less a blur.

The next morning, I was in the bathroom and got yelled at by Daryl Braithwaite, who told me not to use his shampoo. How did he work out that I used it?

At the Q Club, I was becoming a popular figure, dancing away to the big-name bands. A girl approached me and said she wanted to dance on stage with me. Her name was Shelley and I loved her enthusiasm, so I said yes. She would practice doing my dance moves and when we both went on stage, it looked as though we had rehearsed for it, even though I never had to. She was good at imitating me and I liked that I had a fan.

Many people imitated my dance style whenever I went out, and at first I used to feel they were imitating me to make fun of me, but when I heard the saying "imitation is the best form of flattery", I became happy to see them doing my moves.

Shelley and I were soon dancing on both ends of the stage most weekends and meeting lots of interesting artists. We had so much fun performing together and became good friends. We went to see many band members together who we had met at other venues. They usually got us in for free and we would party hard the whole night.

One night at the Q Club, I was asked to dance topless behind a white screen. Everyone working there was coaxing me to do it, so I agreed. I was an easy-going person then – a people pleaser. I just had to just pop a Mandrax tablet whenever I needed to curb my anxiety. Once the effects came on, I became very relaxed. I took off my top and bra and performed my usual moves, arms held high, hair swinging from side to side. With my sensual hip moves and of course my signature ballet turns, you could hear whistles coming from the dance floor. Afterwards, everyone who knew me told me it looked great. A guy from Mushroom records gave me the nickname "Mad Dancer" – it stuck, and from then on people in the industry knew me by that name.

In the summer of 1973, the second Sunbury Festival was on and I wanted to go badly. It was a three-day festival in Sunbury, which seemed very far away.

I asked Mum if I could go and she refused as usual, although that didn't stop me. I easily managed to hitchhike there, as many cars were heading to Sunbury from the main road. I knew that some friends from the Q Club and some male dancers from Nimbin were going to be there.

On arrival, I went to the fenced-off area that led to the stage. I knew one of the bouncers from the Q Club and he let me into the stage area in exchange for a kiss. I was then able to come and go – most of the promoters knew me from the other clubs so they didn't question why I was there.

I knew a lot of the bands playing so I stayed at the front area most of the time, dancing alone or with some of the male dancers, like Benny Zabel. Benny was well known in those days and had a small following of people learning his style.

I danced for hours on end over the whole three days – I guess that's why I was chosen for the cover of the Sunbury Album when it came out.

The following year, in 1974, I just had to go to the Sunbury festival again, as Queen, a new band from the UK, were playing. I had heard that they were sensational! I met some interesting contacts from the previous year, so I was socialising much more

Sunbury 1973

Sunbury 1974

than the first time when I had danced continuously. I was still dancing but getting out and exploring the festival sites more and mingling with the people.

I also had a nose job and felt much more confident. I had a typical Greek nose – okay for a guy, but not for me. I remember being called Ringo sometimes and staring at the mirror for days examining my nose. Eventually my mum saw how disturbed I was about it. She allowed me to have it done after my neighbour told me about her own surgery. She had just had a small set of breasts removed, as she was born with four breasts – two smaller ones under the main ones. In those days, not many people were having plastic surgery so I was a guinea pig.

I went under anaesthetic but was still awake when the surgeon started to use a chisel on my nose. I couldn't yell out that I was still partly conscious, and even though there wasn't pain, the hammering and grinding continued with a sense of breaking. It seemed to go on for ages, until eventually they realised I wasn't fully asleep. To this day, it is always imprinted in my mind and I bring up the incident with the surgeons before I have any procedure done.

The band Queen was hours late coming on stage and the crowd became impatient, egging each other on and booing them. I didn't follow suit – I knew it would be worth the wait, and it was. When the band finally arrived on stage, the crowd told them to get off. The band didn't respond – they didn't flinch a muscle – but got straight into playing. Then Freddie Mercury came on. He was wearing a black jumpsuit and pounded out some great songs! The crowd relaxed and enjoyed the show – the band's performance became the talking point of the concert.

I danced to all my favourite bands – if I didn't like the next band, I would take a break. If I liked all the bands, I would dance all day. I had so much energy to dance and didn't want to miss anything.

I got to meet interesting people from the music industry. A guy named Frank was managing a band called Atlas, who were playing at the festival. Frank became a good acquaintance after Sunbury. He would drop in and see me at my home and we would chat about the band scene. He later got involved with Mushroom and climbed his way up, then later moved on to Frontier Touring, bringing out big acts.

I also knew Michael Gudinski in those days, although he was just an acquaintance. I used to see him a lot at the clubs and he knew me by sight. One night, he invited me to his parents' house to meet a Canadian entrepreneur who he said would promote me. Unfortunately, I was a bit wasted that night. It wasn't a good look and the meeting wasn't successful. I remember the promoter rolling his eyes as if to say "No thanks!" In hindsight, that was a missed opportunity to make it big, although at the time I didn't care because I was a lost soul. Michael never tried to promote me after that night.

I also met Ray Evans, another promoter, and a few others, like Bill Joseph and Steve Hands – all of these guys were big names in the music industry in the mid-70s. It was the best time to be involved in the industry – if you had talent, you could make it a lot more easily in those days. I was starting to become well known in the band scene. I even had a few band members write songs about me. I was totally out there – I was a real party girl!

When the 1973 Sunbury album came out, many people called me to tell me I was on the cover. Although it was a silhouette, there was no mistaking my figure – the long body, long arms, and even the top I was wearing. I remember it was a deep-green top I bought for ten dollars just before the festival. It had an Indian-style print on it and was made of cotton, which cost a lot in those days.

I went home after listening to three days of live music and dancing and was sitting in the lounge room when coverage of the festival was replayed. My younger brother pointed to the screen calling out to everyone at home that I was dancing topless on TV. I retorted, "That's not me, just someone who looks like me!" It was me and they didn't believe me but I wasn't going to admit it.

My older sister was on a date the following week and came back home telling me that I was shown on the big screen, dancing for over a good fifteen minutes in front of the stage. I suppose that was what I would call my fifteen minutes of fame there.

I noticed that a guy in a record store was selling covers of the album years later in a frame. I also saw it advertised Online as well. I thought that, seeing it was my picture, I should have gotten some permission for this – and maybe some royalties? I did call the Mushroom record company and spoke to the head person about it and denied that it was me on the cover – try saying that to everyone that knew me in those days.

There was no mistaking my long arms and body. I wanted to be acknowledged as the Sunbury Dancer but I didn't pursue it any more after that call. When I contacted them about using the photo for the cover of this book decades later they agreed. I was finally acknowledged.

I got more involved in the music scene, my friends and I were getting to know band members on a more personal level and dating some of them.

There was a time when I was about eighteen, I was taken to a house in East St Kilda by a music promoter where a band called AC/DC were staying. They were getting around sixty dollars a week in those days (I overhead them telling a person how much they got).

I would go there often and sit in the lounge area, listening to them talking with all their current girlfriends sitting around. I was usually stoned and stuck to the lounge chair for most of the day. They didn't mind me being there. I don't remember being involved with many of the conversations, I would just nod my head and smile, I guess I was a bit shy then. I only felt confident on the dance floor.

I remember the day Bonn Scott wrote the song 'She's got the Jack'. It was quite a common venereal disease (VD) to get then. It was a very promiscuous time – especially in the band scene – and when he sang it, we just all laughed to ourselves.

There were some other bands staying there at times, one day I saw Stevie Wright come out of his room for a short time to chat to the band members and disappear back to his room. That was the only time I saw him there. He was so cute back then.

I had the flu really bad one time when I was visiting. I was laid out in another room, so sick I couldn't move a muscle. During that time, someone from a band entered the room and had his way with me. I remember being shocked at how he jumped on me and then off in a matter of minutes.

This was something I chose to try and suppress, along with other incidents that happened during the time I was hanging in the band scene. This is the way I dealt with experiences: I repressed them.

Around that time I started mixing with gangsters and dealers that also followed the band scene. There were so many different types of people the music scene attracted, and as I was involved in the scene I was also meeting them and always ready for whatever happened – although I was shy I was always ready for the next adventure despite the risks. The drugs helped.

7

Sydney Nightlife and Encounters

I moved out of my parents' house and was still in Fitzroy. I would drop by to see my mum sometimes when my dad was at work, but I didn't see them often. I stayed with friends, Barbara and Joseph. It was very cheap in those days and I got by doing little jobs.

I had heard from others about how the club scene in Sydney was better than Melbourne during that time, so I decided to go to Sydney on a whim to watch some bands I knew that were playing there. The bands would travel to Sydney to promote themselves and also get a bigger pay packet as well.

It was true. When I arrived in late '74 into early '75 I saw that the nightlife was a buzz – such a fabulous place to be seen at to promote your own talents. I also met lots of famous bands in Sydney. It was such a cosmopolitan city. There were dedicated followers who went to see the bands and travelled from interstate, or the promoters who would then turn them into big class acts either in Australia or overseas.

The two clubs I recall going to were the Whiskey a Go-Go and Chequers. I ended up staying in Sydney for seven months, and during my stay experienced many encounters with drug dealers who frequented those two main clubs. They were notorious in attracting many underground figures – well, that's where I met them.

I met a man at Whiskey a Go-Go called Reggie who was seemingly very nice. I got invited to go to his apartment and hang out with him and his lovely partner either in nearby Kings Cross or at the club. He was half New Zealander or Islander: thick set, fit and a head of black wavy hair, usually tied back. He had huge biceps and worked out a lot. He sometimes performed playing guitar during breaks between bands, other than that he didn't work much from what I saw.

One night he asked me to do him a favour. I nodded back to say I was listening and then he proceeded to tell me that I was to drink with a particular gentleman that he would point out to at the club and I was to say on cue that Reggie was my boyfriend. I didn't understand what he was getting at, but agreed. At the same time I was getting a strange feeling it wasn't right. However, as he was nice to me and always introducing me to people at the club who would buy me drinks, I was okay to do him one favour.

Reggie pointed to an older gentlemen wearing a suit by the bar and told me to sit next to him. I went over and smiled at him, the man was dressed quite conservatively and very pleasant. He was buying me drinks all night. When the music came on, it was too loud to chat so we mainly just drank and nodded at each other through the loud music and focused on watching the live bands. It was always an amazing night there! Whenever I loved a tune I would run up to the dance floor and have a dance on my own, then go back to him when I needed a seat. He was fine with that. After all we just met there, he wasn't my date.

At the end of the night we walked out together onto the street. The club was closing and I was going home when Reggie appeared and looked at me. On cue, I said, "He is my boyfriend." The next moment Reggie started punching into the shocked, inebriated man who was screaming out that he didn't know I was with a guy. He was getting hammered by someone who I thought was a decent person and now showing his true colours. The man fell to the ground and Reggie went through his pockets and took his wallet and then ran off. I was dumbfounded and frozen by what occurred, I soon picked up my legs and left in a hurry because Reggie was yelling at me to go!

The next night, the same man turned up at the club with a few other men in suits, it turned out they were all detectives! He had chosen the wrong man to pick on. The man looked at me but didn't say anything to me, I guess he worked out that Reggie was the instigator and I was just a fool for listening to him – also being very young and naive perhaps saved me. I didn't see Reggie at the club after that. He may have been arrested. Whatever, I never saw him again after that.

There was another time I was out at Chequers and I met an English man in his mid-twenties who reminded me of Robert De Niro; similar in looks, his fit body attracted my attention. He told me his name was Tony and was from Manchester, England, in Sydney on business. He invited me to join him for a smoke at his place. I accepted and went to his lovely one-bedroom apartment that was furnished very expensively with all new fittings and furniture. He was telling me about how he was going to make some investment and get rich from it. I wasn't really listening to the details as I was just enjoying myself, drinking and smoking till the early hours of the morning. I stayed there that night and had fallen asleep on the couch.

When I woke in the morning I noticed Tony was gone. I thought to myself he must have gone to work, I'll just leave, I went to the door but it was locked from the outside. I couldn't get out, I ended up waiting the whole day until he finally came back that evening with take-out food. I ate with him and was telling him how I couldn't get out that morning when he then proceeded to tell me that he wasn't going to let me go until I learn to love him and wanted to be with him. I was shocked by what he said, and as he was a strong looking man knew I had no hope of getting out of there unless I thought of a plan to escape.

His apartment was on a top floor and there were no neighbours to scream out to. I knew I had to go along with him otherwise I would be his prisoner for a long time. Every day I was kept inside and he would leave for the day on business and come home with food later that day. This went on for five or six days until I came up with a plan. By this time, he was getting more comfortable with me and trusting me, I wasn't resisting his advances anymore. He even told me his plans to traffic drugs in a coffin and make $25,000, which was a lot of money then.

Towards the end of the first week of being locked up in his apartment, I suggested that we go out dancing at Chequers for a night out together that weekend. He said he would let me know on the night. I was on my best behaviour and sure I had gained his trust. When I asked again, he agreed we could go out and see a band I had mentioned that I loved.

Come Saturday night, we went to the club hand-in-hand and I pretended to be his girlfriend, kissing him on the cheek at the club to show my affection. I knew I had to follow my plan precisely and not give him any idea of what I was going to do. During the night, I told him I wanted to use the ladies toilet and he walked me to the vicinity of the ladies. I walked down the passage way and then veered to a door that led to a large kitchen area with everyone at work. I entered quickly and asked someone how I could get out the back way. I knew that Tony would be watching the main exits if I disappeared, but he didn't know about the one through the kitchen. I was able to make my escape that night because I knew about the kitchen having an obscure exit leading to the back alley where they dumped the night's rubbish.

I made sure that I didn't go back to Chequers for a while after that incident and stuck to going to Whiskey a Go-Go after that. It was a great place to dance, amazing people and live acts galore. By then I knew a few people working there and after telling them about my ordeal they said, they would look out for me if I needed them anytime. I soon felt safe again.

It wasn't too long after that I met a guy called Paul who I later found out was a dealer of LSD. He was of European-Slavic background, medium build, blonde, very handsome and very generous. He always had an entourage of people around him all the time. He was usually at the bar area with his minders most weekend nights. One night, after watching me dance, he approached to offer me a drink. He told me that he liked how I danced and showed that he liked me too, by wanting to stand with me and buy me drinks all night.

Although there wasn't much talk, it was apparent that we had some connection together. From that night on I started seeing him more often there. I soon became one of his many girlfriends after that. There were two women that hung around his group too – the more authoritative one didn't hesitate telling me that he had a live-in partner too. I was happy to become his girlfriend even after I found out he had many other girlfriends. That didn't sway me from being with him.

I was at one of his homes one day and as usual he had many other men congregating there too. He was never alone, he left me in the bedroom that day for hours and I was a bit bored so I started looking through his draws and in one of them there was a revolver. I quickly closed the draw in fear. When Paul came in I pretended I hadn't seen it – but from that day on I was a bit scared of who he was. He told me he hated heroin and saw how it destroyed lots of people's lives, and threatened he would hurt me if I ever took it.

I didn't tell Paul that a month later, one of the men that worked for him tricked me into going with him. With the understanding we were going to see Paul, I had followed this guy into a hotel room in King's Cross, where he jabbed a needle filled with heroin in my arm and then raped me – afterwards threatening to kill me if I told Paul what happened. I chose to keep it to myself. I wanted to tell Paul but I knew the threat was real and if I told Paul, then he would maybe hurt both of us. It was best to repress that along with all the other hurts I had experienced. One more I could deal with.

I didn't have anywhere to stay at times and Paul took me to a place near King's Cross to stay with another female friend. He had previously taken me to another female friend's place and I stayed there for a couple of weeks, hardly doing much except eating what was in the fridge and watching TV. He did care for me and was always there when I needed his help.

At the second place in Potts Point I met his friend Faye who was very nice to me, I think Paul gave her some money to take care of me as she was very generous and I shared her room without any problems. There were strange people staying in the huge house where rooms were being rented out, however all the people there were friends. Every weekend there were LSD tripping parties held there. I went to a few whilst I was there.

The first time I took an LSD trip I saw a guy doing acrobatics down the stairs at that house. Whenever I took LSD, I usually would be dancing like a ballerina for up to twelve hours at the parties where every person played a role. It was like a part of them came out during that time that they kept hidden otherwise.

I was thinking of going back to Melbourne because life, although fun, was a struggle. I wasn't eating properly and I was always trying to scrape together money. I decided to pack just as I had taken an LSD trip. For the next eight hours I was focused on folding my clothes and placing them in my suitcase as neatly as possible. Once I came down off the trip and looked at my clothes folded in the case it was as though they were brand new, so well folded – there wasn't a crease and they looked like art, that's how well I folded them. I didn't leave after that. I had a change of mind.

There was also an incident when I had met a girl from overseas named Anja in Melbourne who then came to visit me in Sydney. She also wanted to experiment and try out LSD, but she ended up having a bad experience from it. The guy downstairs – who I got the chills from – had given her the trip, I later found out.

She was staying with me in the shared room for a while, and we both had gotten pregnant from a couple of guys we met together that didn't believe in condoms and we weren't on the pill. The next day we went to the doctors to get the 'after pill' – a tablet you take that makes you bleed so much that you lose the embryo.

Anja was further along with her pregnancy than I was (the guy downstairs may have gotten to her first and she didn't tell me). She ended up aborting a foetus fully-formed into the toilet and leaving Sydney worse for wear from the experience. I'll never forget looking in the toilet and seeing the foetus all red and already forming into a tiny baby before being flushed down.

At the parties at the Potts Point house, most of the residents were taking drugs. The ones who didn't would securely lock their doors on the particular nights, as what went on was so surreal and at times comical and fun when we got together to party.

On some trips I would look at the walls moving and melt into the colours of a picture; a three-dimensional experience of beauty opened by the brain using it's capabilities to see beyond. I could be entertained by just sitting back and experiencing whatever my mind opened up to. There were times I just listened to Stevie Wonder or popular seventies music on my own and just be blissed out on the couch, the music soaring through my body and the psychedelic colours that would emerge from an object or a picture was enough to entertain me for hours.

There was a Greek man at one of the tripping parties one night who knew Paul. He kept saying to me "What do you reckon?" every time he walked past. I was very puzzled as to what he meant by that – after all, I was young and naive. I still didn't get it until the morning when he finally blurted out what he was hinting at – sex, of course.

There was a night when we were all together in the main living area on LSD. It was unusually cold; there was no heating except in the bedrooms, so one of the men doing the acrobatics made his way downstairs and decided to break up the furniture and put in the fireplace. He went into the kitchen first, then the living area to break up the wooden chairs to use as firewood. When he had used them all up, I wondered what else he would put the axe to. This guy had an unusual name, Vivian, he and his friend Steve must have been dealers or into something crooked. He was staying at the house for a few weeks in one of the rooms.

I went out with Faye and them one night and it was clearly not a good idea. The guys somehow had gotten hold of a Kombi van from someplace and drove us miles away to a remote area. There were green plastic bags of dresses and pants that were packed into a cupboard. I found them during the night when Vivien and his friend left us in the van in a dark cold place all night. We were freezing to death, as we didn't have blankets, there was no heating in the van and it was the middle of winter in some remote area. We were shivering so much and that's when I decided to look through the cupboards and found the clothes. I took many of them out of the bags and threw them on us, all the while wondering whose clothes they were. In the morning, Vivian and his friend turned up. We knew we couldn't berate them for leaving us all night. We were scared of who they were by now, just happy to get back home and safe.

I took a step back from these guys and made sure I didn't go anywhere with them after that night. I heard some whispers about them being robbers, dealers with guns and eventually they just left the house suddenly. Don't know where they went but I sure was relieved, the stories were starting to spook me.

The guy who rented out the rooms was a dealer. I didn't know that until we were raided. He always wore overalls, medium framed guy with shoulder length hair that was very fine and he had a very thin face. I thought he was just the janitor or the caretaker of the place.

One other man living there always looked like a demon to me whenever I was high on something. He lived downstairs and I distinctly saw horns coming out of his head every time I was high. It sure was a warning to me to stay away from him! He was spooky and I did keep away from him as much as possible. His eyes had such a darkness in them and he gave me the feeling that he had no soul. My intuition was always screaming to me to stay away from him. Even when he was nice to me, he seemed dangerous!

I was going home one night after returning from Chequers and I knocked on the basement flat as I didn't have a key. To my surprise a group of men in black suits had come to the door with guns in their hands drawn towards me. Thank God I was recognised by the man who ran the place and I was then able to enter safely.

There were also times I walked to the house during the day and even at night and noticed lots of police cars or strange men watching the place. I thought to myself it was just my imagination and thought nothing of it until one day the whole street was closed off and everyone in the house was detained. My girlfriend Faye and I were questioned and because of my ignorance of what was going on they let my friend and I go, as she had nothing to do with them either. They told us we had to go and stay with her mum in Newcastle, so we got a lift there and all I remember was eating non-stop for two weeks at her Mum's place, then leaving. That was the last time I ever saw her or Paul.

8

Back in Melbourne

Once I got back to Melbourne in 1975, I stayed temporarily at my parents' home in Fitzroy. Within a matter of days, I was itching to go out dancing again. I heard about a small dance hall near my area so went for a walk there one evening to check it out. It was there I watched a new band called Split Enz, from New Zealand. They were a zany-looking bunch of guys who were brightly dressed!

I liked the sound of them, so I soon got up to have a dance on my own and was improvising to their unusual sounding tunes. When the show finished, I met the pianist, Eddie, who came over to me to comment on my dancing. We had a nice conversation and before he left he took my number and said he would call me whenever he came to Melbourne to perform. The crowds grew bigger each time the band came back to Melbourne.

I did go to a couple of their gigs when they came back to play in Melbourne later that year and saw Eddie again. He was a quiet type, had a soft nature, slim, average height, clean cut and well spoken. I did enjoy his company and always danced to show my support for them.

He was such a nice guy that I was hoping to be his girlfriend after seeing him a few times, however one evening I invited one of my girlfriends to come along to meet him and they both hit it off. He seemed enamoured with her and asked for her number, dumping me for her without any warning. I think they both were feeling sorry for me later on because they invited me to go with them to a gig in Sydney. I went, but was feeling a bit upset seeing them together, so I decided to leave the venue and hunt out another place to have a dance.

When Eddie finished his concert, my girlfriend pointed out that I had disappeared and they panicked when they couldn't see me anywhere in the club. They were worried about me all night and were looking everywhere. When I returned to the hotel room the next day, they were upset at me for not telling them where I went. I had gone out dancing and ended up with the manager of a night club I met. He gave me free drinks all night once I got onto the dance floor. We later went back to his place, and this was my way of getting back at Eddie for dumping me. After that I didn't see Eddie again.

9

Warning Signs

In 1976, one night after I was out partying hard with one of my girlfriends, I ended up going back to her place to sleep it off. This particular night I fell out of the bed (I had overindulged again), and opened my eyes to a vision by the bedroom door. I saw a dark, olive-skinned man who was tall, slim, wearing a dark suit and a black top hat. It reminded me of the Undertaker in those old black and white movies I used to watch on television. I associated that man with Death and this is why I was scared after seeing him! I started rubbing my eyes in disbelief at what I was seeing. This man was just standing there gazing straight at me and it felt like death had visited me. I was very afraid of the vision, but I was so loaded with alcohol and pills that I soon fell asleep again, once I lifted myself off the floor and went back to bed.

In the morning I asked my friend if her mum had a boyfriend staying over, to which she replied "No. Why?" I immediately realised that it was a warning to me that if I kept going this way, I wouldn't survive much longer abusing my body through drugs and alcohol.

A doctor in Sydney had supplied me with Mandrax a few times as I had given him so many stories as to why I needed the pills, he eventually gave in to my pleading and gave me a prescription. He was a kind doctor who also gave me fatherly advice, saying that if I kept going on this destructive path in a couple of years my life would spiral out of control with consequences. He gave me two years to live at the pace I was going. I was quite a wreck with all the partying I did, there were many late nights where at times I hardly slept for days unless I crashed on someone's couch.

This statement gave me some truth to how my life was spiralling downwards and I could now see how destructive it was. My whole life was based around dancing and partying, because of the scene I was in, from consuming alcohol and popping pills. I already had news that a few of my friends had overdosed on those pills then and it contributed to their deaths and I heard there were many others too. I called a gay friend of mine to invite him over and his mum answered and said, "Oh, you didn't hear, he overdosed last night and passed away." People started saying that because Mandrax was contributing to many deaths it would be taken off the market soon, but that didn't happen until some years later.

I personally had taken too many Mandrax pills a couple of times and luckily was rushed to hospital to get my stomach pumped. I was also starting to meet people who had progressed into taking the hard drugs and tempting me to follow them. Luckily my preference was more for pills, although I would sometimes snort heroin when I was out with new friends at a house gathering.

I even had a boyfriend in South Yarra who offered me heroin rocks to smoke every time I went to see him. He was selling it too, because there were always people there asking to try the product. I was well aware of his dealings and eventually, I guess, remembered what Paul had told me about the dangers of the drug, I decided to move on from that relationship. It didn't involve dancing so I soon tired of visiting him, smoking and going to bed high.

The statement by the doctor ran through my thoughts more often, thoughts about death and the warning sign of the apparition at my girlfriend's had scared me as well. My life wasn't getting better with drugs, I was heading for trouble as my needs for more drugs required more money. I was just surviving. Guys I dated would pay for things and I was dependant on others. Sometimes I would go hungry. Other times I was on top of the world living the high life. I felt like life was a roller coaster, I was starting to do things to sell my soul. I was getting addicted to taking Mandrax, and started visiting different doctors to get scripts. Sometimes I was successful, other times not.

I went to my visit my local doctor in my area in desperation one day for a script, as my supply was finished and I was getting withdrawal symptoms. I was very stunned at what occurred that day. I had visited him many times previously for the usual needs, like flu medicine or antibiotics. I felt he was a stern man because of his serious manner. He was Indian and in those days I didn't know many people from that country – actually, he was one of the first Indian doctors I had visited. The Clinic was in Smith Street, Collingwood.

On this occasion, I meekly told him that I needed a script for the pills because I couldn't sleep. That was my excuse. He asked me to lie on the table and went off somewhere. He came back minutes later with a condom and after dropping his trousers, jumped onto the table, having removed my panties hastily. I was so surprised as this happened so fast! I didn't have time to even think about it. I put my pants back on and jumped off, dazed at what happened. The doctor proceeded to his desk and I followed him, he wrote me a script for the pills and a repeat script to keep me quiet. I never went back there ever again after that incident.

There was a time that I had a badly sprained ankle before this incident occurred and I had gone to see this doctor to attend to it. He wasn't available to see me that day and there was another doctor on duty. He asked me what was my problem and I told him about my sore ankle. He then proceeded to rub my breasts with cupped hands once I sat down on a chair next to his desk in his room. I thought that was odd, being very naive I was puzzled as to why he did that, but was very embarrassed to tell anyone about it after.

I was at a low point in my life and would do almost anything to numb myself with pills. This was getting out of control. I was using my body more to get my needs met. I slept around, mainly with band members who could offer me drugs in exchange for a good time. I enjoyed the scene so much that it didn't bother me. I was always meeting members of great bands and invited to parties and getting high. Dancing kept me going, being acknowledged and being seen for who I was.

It was the culmination of all the experiences and how I overdosed a couple of times that led me to question my life, and of course the warning from the kind doctor in Sydney. That was what cemented my determination to make changes for myself. I so wanted to meet a gentleman one day and have a life filled with love. I adored the classic love stories on TV and day dreamed that I was a lost princess.

I decided soon after if an opportunity arose for me to get out of Melbourne I would leave as soon as possible. I knew where I wanted to go and that was London, where the men in bowler hats resided. In the meantime, I had met new people and was soon hanging out with girls who were either strippers or escorts that I met through the social scene of drugs. Sometimes when I was bored, I would go and visit them and get high with them.

There was a time when a girlfriend was offered a stripping job at the Puckapunyal army barracks and she couldn't make it. She had committed to another job that night. It was paying two hundred dollars, but fifty would go towards the guy who would drive you there and be your bodyguard. In those days, they paid one hundred and fifty dollars to dance topless for about twenty minutes, plus the extra ten minutes that was wasted on setting up. This was so much more than I could earn from a wage, so when she offered it to me I accepted.

On the evening of the job, the bouncer came to pick me up and explained how it went. All I had to do was wear a sexy bikini bottom and take off my bra and dance. I thought well that's not hard to do, I already danced topless behind the screen at Q Club and that was for free too! He drove me to the barracks and we entered a large room with many men all in casual clothing waiting for my arrival. I felt somewhat shy but my magic pill was starting to work and I was starting to relax. I was introduced to the sergeant who was celebrating an event and I remember he just turned thirty-five years old. It must have been a gift from the men for his birthday!

The bouncer brought in a small music player and played some music for me to dance to – easy. I went around the formed circle of men and danced, swaying and dancing, as erotic as I thought a stripper would dance. I wasn't trained but I sure knew what to do. I was a hit with them all, whistles and laughter soon broke out. The sergeant was seated in the middle and I had to go and give him a little tease of a dance, he was a real gentleman, didn't grope me at all. I guess having a bodyguard was a good idea after all – imagine if I went alone? Time went quickly and before I knew it, the music was switched off and I was back in the car driving back home. It was my first and last time stripping.

I heard stories of how a lot of the strippers started being raffled off after they performed. I didn't want to do that, so I didn't go down that path, even though it was easy money. I was always tempted to deviate, however the universe always seemed to slap me in the face to find obstacles to stop me and it worked. I also did have a conscience too, and was terrified in case my dad found out. I had many reasons to stop me going any further, but my father was the main one!

One of the houses I used to visit was run by shady characters, where some of the girls worked as escorts. There was a particular man who dropped by to see the owners at times, and I would chat to him innocently when I dropped in for a visit. I had met them through the club scene, and we soon became friendly enough to catch up for drinks and smoke on the weekends. They were great fun to be with! I would drop by whenever I was around the area and stay a few hours, have a joint then head off home after. There were always people dropping in so they didn't mind me coming by.

One day, I was leaving to go home and this guy asked me if I wanted a lift home. I didn't hesitate to say yes, as I was only too happy to get a ride. What happened on the way took me by surprise, though. After a few minutes in the car (an old Falcon), we had police cars chasing us and I was starting to get worried. The next few minutes were so surreal. He took out a rifle from under his seat and started to aim it out the window at the police. He wrapped a large type of hanky across his face like a bandit and stopped the car and was then yelling at the police. He got out of his car with me, as we were being surrounded by them. They had stopped and gotten out of their cars, and were ready to have a shoot-out. That's when I realised how dangerous it was.

He was shouting out to them that he had a hostage. I guess this got their attention and they decided to let us go then. They left quickly and this man drove me back to the house without any excuses or apologies. He just dropped me back to where I was in the beginning and was his usual self, smiling and chatting like nothing happened.

I had taken a barbiturate tablet that day, and because I was numb already I was able to cope with what happened without being emotional. Afterwards, I knew I had to do something about my life, I was attracting so many negative experiences and I felt ready to make a change.

I met an English group called The Foundations that were touring in Melbourne, and that gave me the opportunity to leave. I got to know one of the band members on the night they played and he told me he lived in London. That word lit up in my head. This was the sign I was looking for to change my life. I became quite excited to hear about London and his band. He offered me a place to stay if I ever decided to go and visit. I decided then and there – this was my opportunity to get out of this scene now.

The next time (which turned out to be the last time) I went to visit my close friend John and his girlfriend turned out to be a dreadful night, I had gotten wasted and was lying in bed with them. I loved him dearly, we were very close. I had met him when he was working and straight, now fast forward a year and he was starting to rely heavily on heroin (initially it was just pills) and was now trying to tempt me to join him. He tempted his girlfriend to join him on his downhill journey and she obliged.

I knew then that I was losing them to the heroin. I felt their souls being consumed by darkness. The drug was evil because of what it did to people, and how they ended up doing anything to maintain their habits. In that state they didn't comprehend the enormity of their actions and the end result, ultimately leading to jail, death or battling their inner demons, a journey through hell back to healing, which can take many years.

I was lucky that I resisted joining them, but knew that if I joined them, maybe I wouldn't survive. They were mixing it with pills and alcohol. It wasn't fun anymore, they just wanted to stay in bed after taking a hit and lie in bed for a couple of days. By now they had both lost their jobs and were getting desperate for money. This only made me more determined that I was going to save myself and leave that life.

I loved my dancing so much that the thought of just staying in bed doing nothing was enough to deter me from entering that dark place. I was already addicted to taking Mandrax, but was able to still get out and dance although the effects would soon catch up. I would eventually go into a deep sleep after coming off the high and end up sleeping as long as a day and night at times.

The next day I decided I would buy a one way cheap ticket to London to leave as soon as possible. I was going to leave everything behind, all my friends, all my contacts. I spoke with my mum that next morning, telling her I needed to leave and save myself. She understood and gave me the money to help me out with the ticket. I promised to call her whenever I could and I did at every opportunity. I would always grab any opportunity to call mum. If I was staying over at someone's house, I'd ask in my sweetest voice if I could call my mum for a few minutes. That was usually okay by them. In those days calling international was very expensive. I would just call and say hi and tell her that I was okay and doing well. I knew Mum worried a lot about me, so at least I could do this for her.

10

London

I arrived in London in the spring of the year 1976. I was this young and vulnerable teenager, who didn't know anything about London except for the men in bowler hats that I had seen on television. I immediately went to the phone booth and contacted the guy I had met in Melbourne touring at that time from The Foundations' band. I was lucky that he answered the phone. I had only given him short notice before leaving Australia. Once I bought the ticket, I called him to tell him I was coming to London. I was, after all, very spontaneous, and would just take off whenever I wanted – a free spirit.

He instructed me on how to get from the airport to his house, which was located in Shepherd's Bush and after some time managed to find it with public transport and his directions. On arrival at his door, he greeted me with a smile. I guess he was happy to see me. He then showed me where I would be sleeping that night. I looked up at the rows of bunk beds, and he nodded and said, that his three other brothers slept there – all in the same room! They were at school now and his parents were at work.

I decided I needed to find my own place to stay at. I wasn't going to share with four guys in a room. I dumped my bags and had a quick nap on one of the empty bunk beds, while he had work to do in the living area with his band. Feeling more refreshed a few hours later, he invited me to go with him to a recording studio. They were trying out for backing singers that day and he asked if I wanted to try out as well. Being so insecure and frightened by the thought of being rejected I said no – even though I had been told I had a good voice by some guys I dated that had heard me sing whilst in the car going for long drives. I would always sing along to what was on the radio. I had even taken singing lessons in Melbourne at the Melba Conservatory thinking I could become a back-up singer one day. My dad paid for two terms then stopped paying. I was very disappointed at first, later I went and found other teachers to have lessons with. I did have a secret yearning to sing, but as I wasn't confident in myself I didn't go further with it.

Towards the evening and back at the house, I told him I was going into Mayfair to find a particular club I had heard of, so I hailed a cab after taking the bus closer to the city area. I noticed the cabbie was very friendly asking me lots of questions during the ride when I recognised a landmark again. I realised he was ripping me off! He knew I was new to London so he tried to make some extra money. I have to admit I had a couple of drinks at the house before leaving. I had bought a duty-free bottle of bourbon and wanted to unwind before I left for the club.

I paid four pounds for a ride that was really only a few blocks away from where I hailed him.

I approached the entrance of the club, called Gullivers, and was flatly refused entry by an older, well-dressed man. He was the doorman. I pleaded for him to let me go in, and it was only when I told him I was from Australia that he reluctantly agreed to let me in, 'just this once'.

I heard that many famous band members frequented that club, but the only one I ever saw was Lionel Richie. There were, however, lots of rich Arabs, mainly there on holidays or for business. This was the time when oil was aplenty and so many of the Gulf States became extremely rich from the oil drilling finds, and the people from the regions were looked after generously by their government. London was flooded with many Arabic men and families.

There were lots of Arabic men frequenting the clubs around that time. I was meeting loads of men from every region of the Gulf. I found that they were very nice to me and felt very comfortable in their company. Once I hit the dance floor that was it, I would dance all night, I had men bringing me drinks, dancing with me, even offering me smoke of hash already rolled when I clearly became a regular of the club.

There was one guy called Moosa that was always there – a local, I think. He may have been a dealer. I was on the dance floor as usual one night and he placed a cube of hashish in my hand and told me to have it. I had never taken it in this form so I gobbled it up, I didn't realise how strong it was. I was floored by it. I actually fell into a heap on the dance floor and was eventually carried off and placed in an obscure dark part of the club and attended to by Moosa and his friends until I was able to get back on my feet hours later. I later discovered that the cube was enough hash to get a few people stoned on with – I took it all myself. I sure learnt the hard way how to take it!

My first night in London I had met an older African-American man called Basil at Gullivers. I told him how I just arrived that morning and was looking for a room. He then told me that he knew of a place that had a room to rent out in Putney. I immediately told him I was very eager to go and see the room as soon as possible. He suggested the next day was good for him. I decided to stay out all night until 7am, then go to a nearby café to meet him early in the morning.

That café was a popular place to go in Soho and later when I settled in London after a few months, this became a place I would frequent with my girlfriends after clubbing all night. One night after being out till the early hours of the morning, my friends and I went there and George Best, the famous soccer player, came over to say hello to some guy on our table and then nodded to us. It was a popular place to be, you didn't know who would drop in.

Basil turned up and drove me to an area called Fulham, very close to Putney Bridge. The owner of the building opened the door on his way out, he quickly introduced himself and let us in. He was a pilot, I heard. Basil took me to the room. It was a tiny room, which had only a single bed and a chair in it. I had never seen such a small room in my life, but it didn't matter. I was more interested in having my own room than the size of it. I had my own place to sleep in now. I was introduced to the two other English women I would be sharing with who were much older – one a nurse, another was working in an office. They were happy to have me stay after a quick interview and once I paid the deposit and rent, I went back to get my belongings. This was the start of my adventures in London.

11

Memorable London Dates

During my first weeks in London, I met a tall, dark man with long dreadlocks on a busy shopping strip. He approached me after following me for a few minutes, and asked me lots of questions about who I was and where I came from.

I didn't feel intimidated by his presence – after all, he was zanily dressed and looked like a musician in a reggae band.

Immediately after asking about myself, he wanted to tell me about his friend Issam, who was a great guy. He asked if I would like to meet him, as he was on his way there.

I was happily chatting to him when he casually pulled out a golden revolver and swirled it around his fingers, showing off. He laughed when he saw the worried look on my face, saying, "Don't worry."

I nodded, feeling unsure about this guy, but as he was a smooth talker I agreed to meet Issam. After all, I was new to London and needed to make some friends.

He took me to an apartment complex with a doorman and security in the lifts. After pressing the code, he brought me up to the 12th floor. He was greeted by a balding, thirty-five-year-old man, who was fit, very confident, and comfortable in his skin.

They spoke for a couple of minutes, then he said goodbye and disappeared back into the lift. I was wondering what was going on, when Issam invited me into his home. He was very cordial, offering me a drink and a seat opposite him in a very impressive furnished place – a penthouse, as it was the only apartment on the 12th floor.

He asked me a few questions about myself and relaxed into his armchair. I liked his manner, feeling that he could possibly become a friend.

After our first meeting, Issam told me I was welcome to drop by, but it was best to call first. I felt confident enough and started dropping in to see him every week or two.

He was very helpful, asking me if I was okay and telling me to let him know if I needed anything.

I didn't know much about his private life, and didn't ask. I guessed what he did for work as I saw the extent of his wealth over time. He was Saudi Arabian, well educated, and his home was in London. His limousine driver drove a Bentley, which was a beautiful black car. One day, I was waiting outside Harrods for transport home, when his driver pulled up to offer me a ride. I was thrilled! I felt like a millionaire, sitting in the back being driven by a chauffeur wearing a hat.

Issam had different cars for every day of the week and owned a helicopter. I had seen his fast sporty cars drive up while I was waiting for him in the lobby – sometimes for a couple of hours, if I didn't organise to meet beforehand. I was enamoured with him because of his wealth and how well he treated me, as he was such a kind and generous man.

He was very secretive, and one night he told me he was going to fly to Belfast for business. I started to think that maybe he was making some lucrative black-market deal, but I wasn't sure as he never told me much.

After he got to know me, he would openly chat about general matters, but never about his work. He was more of a listener than a talker.

I noticed that he had placed a framed photo of me on his mantelpiece with a few other women. I was surprised to see it on display, because it was a fantastic picture of me and I didn't know he had taken it.

I saw that I was one of many women, so decided not to get attached to him. I didn't think he wanted a relationship anyway, as he was so busy making deals on the phone or meeting people to talk about business matters.

He did help me out one time when I was stuck without accommodation. I had been wearing the same clothes for a few days while I was sleeping on someone's couch, and had to leave in the morning when they went to work. My clothes were in a suitcase, held hostage by the owner of a bedsitter where I had overstayed by a couple of days – he wanted a week's rent before he would release it back to me.

I called Issam and he told me to come to his apartment. Once I arrived, he told me to go and have a bath as I looked a bit scruffy for his liking.

The spacious bathroom had a huge, gold-plated bath with fancy taps. I added bubble bath to the water and soaked in it for a long time in a blissful state. He then brought me some clothes to change into, gave me money and told me he was waiting on someone, so I had to leave. I didn't mind because I was clean and could afford to go to a hotel that night and buy a sumptuous meal there, pay to get my suitcase back and look for a room to rent.

The hotel staff were surprised I was dining alone and commented on how I was too attractive to be there by myself.

I never believed men when they complimented me because I thought they were only trying to seduce me. I never took compliments seriously unless it was about dancing.

Eventually, I introduced my new flatmate to Issam. She had constantly nagged me, wanting to meet him after hearing me talk about his kindness, generosity, apartment, and fast cars. They started seeing each other while I was away visiting Bahrain again; I didn't mind as I wasn't a possessive type.

One day in the lift he told me, "You are the salt of the Earth." I felt he meant it, and always kept it in my heart.

Issam also took me to his cousin's restaurant, which was designed to look like a cave. Materials were superimposed onto to the brickwork and painted to resemble a real cave. They had delicious Arabic food and live music, usually during the evening on weekends.

His cousin was always happy to see me, welcomed me to sit and eat, and told me I could drop in whenever I was in the area. I took up the offer a few times. I knew Issam wanted to make sure I had somewhere to go if I was ever hungry, and that's why he took me there. I felt safe knowing that he was concerned and looking out for me.

I met Suri when I stayed a short time as a bedsitter in an area of London called Victoria. A friend had a couple of weeks left on the bedsit, so let me use it as she didn't need it anymore.

The area was close to a major train station, and had a small cinema nearby. I went there one day to watch a movie and a few men wearing raincoats made odd rustling sounds. I was the only female there. I didn't dare go back after that.

One day, I had to get some medicine. I walked into a small pharmacy and approached the pharmacist to ask for his advice on what I should take. He was very chatty and asked me about myself. I told him I was new to London and staying nearby. He then asked if he could take me out to dinner and I agreed, as he was quite a handsome Anglo-Indian in his early twenties.

Suri contacted me and took me out one evening to a club called Annabel's, which I've heard is still running today. He told me he had to pay a hefty fee to join and apparently was one of the first people of colour to become a member in the prestigious club.

I had a grand time drinking and dancing with all the English couples dressed in their finery.

I saw Suri quite a few times in the beginning; however, I did travel back and forth to Bahrain later and had a few dancing opportunities with the Arabic band I had met at a party.

When I contacted him again after a while away – travelling mainly to Bahrain – he told me he had moved to Sloane Street, behind Harrods in Knightsbridge.

I went to visit him there and he told me that famous people came for their scripts and shopped for cosmetics, including Princess Diana and royalty from Saudi Arabia.

I was there one time as he was serving an Arab man and quoting him a figure I thought was a little excessive for scripts. Suri explained, "They can afford it – if they're true bloodline Saudis and they're traveling for medical reasons, the government pays for everything. They cover all their medical fees and hotels."

Suri was making big money so close to the 5-star Carlton Towers hotel where the Arabic visitors stayed. He was only a few doors away.

He had a basement beneath the shop with designer make up and perfumes and told me that I could help myself, as they were all samples. There was so much to choose from, but as I wasn't into make up. I just took a Chanel No. 5 perfume. It was my favourite for a long time.

Time passed and we only saw each other when I was in the area, as I moved away and had other adventures.

I did encounter him a couple of times after many years elapsed – one time at the Dubai horse racing. It was a surprise to bump into him there. He asked if I remembered his nickname. It was "Snake".

He lived his life fully and I always remember him for the fun times out and lavish lifestyle.

We reconnected through Facebook Messenger during the Covid lockdown, and sometimes we briefly have a chat.

12

Mayfair and Soho Clubs

Gullivers was a fantastic club, it was best to go later when the music was pumping later in the night. So, before that I used to go to Pip's Wine Bar nearby in Mayfair. I was told it had a popular champagne bar section. I went there often and sat at the champagne area and would be offered free glasses of champagne from the male patrons, once I told them I was visiting from Australia. Some also had recognised me from Gullivers. They only served Dom Perignon champagne and it was so easy to drink, as it was so smooth on the palate. I soon got to meet lots of people there who went on to Gullivers club afterwards, and I also started getting a lot of dating offers.

At Gullivers I would mainly be seen most of the night on the dance floor, dancing freely. People always made sure I had enough room to express myself. I soon had some admirers jumping in to dance with me, the doorman never refused me entry after the first night.

I knew a few Algerian men who used to come into the club and wanted to date me. On one particular night, two men I knew both tried to pursue me at the same time to go out with them afterwards. They were trying so hard to get me as their date and it got to the point that they felt they had to fight for me. Before I knew it, there were chairs flying everywhere, the whole place broke into a fight. It was a mess. The two men inflamed the situation and more people started to fight. I left the club whilst it was happening as it was out of control and people were leaving in a hurry.

The next night, I was told by the doorman the men that started the fight over me were barred for life and I nearly was too, but they decided they liked my dancing too much to do that. The regulars liked me there. Besides that, business was booming! The two men had caused a lot of damage to the place and they had to pay for the damages as well as being barred. Luckily, they both worked for the Algerian Government and had good positions and were able to pay for the repairs.

During my time in London I also used to go to the La Valbonne Club, which was extremely spacious in size, in central London. I loved being there, especially towards the end of the night when I had a chance to claim the dance floor. Earlier, it was usually jam-packed with patrons of all nations, smartly dressed. It was all class there. La Valbonne had a French restaurant inside and at times I'd get invited to join some rich Arab dining there and could try out some exotic meals. I remember how I tried escargot for the first time there, I ate it thinking how rubbery it tasted. I don't think I ordered snails ever again. I indulged in drinking the French champagne, and sometimes my girlfriends on my insistence were able to join us to have some champagne too.

I met an English man from the London Ballet Company there one night who offered me a job with the Company. He had seen me dancing for some time on the dance floor and approached me as soon as I took a break. He was in his forties and dressed in a black skivvy and black pants. He was appealing to me, he looked like such a gentleman. I drank and chatted with him that whole night whilst he told me all about the ballet and where they travelled to and expressed how I could join them on their travels abroad. I was interested in joining the ballet, but when he told me the pay, I decided it wasn't worth the effort. I was having the time of my life now anyway. Later, I did see the missed opportunity there, and it wasn't my first.

I had another offer from a talent scout who asked me whether I could sing as well as dance. This lady was a regular at Gullivers and wanted to promote me. She told me she could make me a star. I didn't even go for the audition she offered me. I just shrugged my shoulders and went back onto the dance floor.

The La Valbonne Club became my favourite club, and I lost interest in going to Gullivers. I usually went with two girlfriends Julie and Dawn who I had met at a guy's place one day. They had just come to London from the countryside and needed a place to stay. I moved in with an English girl, Frances, for a couple of weeks. After the first week she decided to go and live in Paris and left suddenly. I often wondered what happened to her after I came back home to Australia. I was watching an English documentary a few years ago about escorts and recognised her. Frances had become a high-class escort and this documentary was based on her life. I saw that she was quite well off financially, driving a Jaguar car and dressed elegantly. Although she looked happy, I reflected on my own experiences and wondered whether her soul could be happy.

The owner of the bedsitter I stayed at started coming to my door and annoying me. He would try to kiss me and chased me around the room until I screamed for him to leave me alone. He would then back off and try again when he was around the area again. It was good timing when I met Julie and Dawn and having a spare bed I offered them a place to stay for free with me. They were good company and maybe a deterrent for the owner as well. Although he still tried with us on other occasions, we managed to push him out quicker together. The girls stayed with me for a short time, we had lots of fun going out dancing together. They had met a couple of Persian men one day so they moved on. I eventually lived with them later on in Earls Court for six months before I travelled back home to Australia

I met a guy called BJ, an African-American friend of Basil's, who was a smooth talker and, I would say, a ladies' man with all the benefits from it! I went out with him a few times and he was always dressed immaculately in a suit. He was tall, dark and handsome. He had all the woman after him and he took advantage of his appealing looks to live in luxury provided by them. I wasn't rich enough for him so he didn't pursue me for long, once he knew about my finances being almost zilch, but he liked me enough to call me sometimes to check on me and inquire about how my life was going.

I remember meeting an Iranian guy at the nightclub one night and he asked me to come along to his friend's place where he was staying in Knightsbridge and have some drinks. When I got there, I couldn't believe my eyes! I asked to use the toilet there and was on my way upstairs when I saw BJ. He was shocked to see me as well. I told him I was just hanging out, nothing more, and he then preceded to explain how he met this guy and had offered him a room even though the place belonged to a princess from a Gulf State. She was away for the month and BJ was looking after it and making some money on the side. He was making money from all angles: this guy must have been paying him some money for staying as well as becoming a rich contact for him.

Around that time I also met a couple of men from Bahrain. One was the son of a big business man who had many clubs in Bahrain. I eventually visited him and saw the extent of his wealth. One other man I met in London was named Issa, a Persian born in Bahrain. Issa was the first man who invited me to visit him in his country, and that is how my fascination for the Gulf grew and where I had the most memorable and exciting times of my life.

13

Bahrain
– The Pearl in the Gulf

When Issa (a young Cat Stevens lookalike) invited me to visit Bahrain after we met in London, I accepted. He paid for my ticket and I hopped on the first available plane there from London. In those days Gulf Air was a very popular airline and maybe the only one flying for that region then. I remember being on that plane when they hit an air pocket and the plane started descending at a rapid speed – that was scary stuff!

I arrived at the airport, a very old and small one at that time. There were guards carrying rifles, something I had never seen before. They wore red berets and full uniform, some of them had their jackets off, as it was scorching hot when I stepped off the plane.

The immigration officials weren't fluent in English and had difficulty asking why I was visiting. Luckily Issa appeared and spoke to them and they let me through. I went to his family home, met his sisters and his mother and brother-in law who was bringing in immigrants into Bahrain to work from India. I don't know whether it was legit and I didn't care.

Once I settled in with the family, I found out that Issa was already engaged with another Bahraini girl so I decided that I wasn't going to have anything to do with him anymore, I started going out with his older sister who owned a hairdresser business, compliments of her Saudi Arabian older boyfriend. She was also dating a law enforcement officer of high ranking. Every Friday they took me to fabulous parties held by the rich and famous. I was quite popular with the Gulf people and I blended in well with the culture. I watched some of the women dance to the live band that always seemed to appear at everything I went to with Issa's sister. The main band member, Mohammed Ali, was a large-framed, lovely person and one of the best-known singers around.

The Sheikh I met at these parties always invited the band to all these parties he attended and he paid them well. I loved all the attention, food, drinks, company and all the money I was getting just to dance! This was my dream come true, dancing and getting rewarded for it. The Sheikh was a high official, related to the Royal Family and I kept bumping into him everywhere I went. He loved my dancing too and many times he gave me money when he saw me dance.

I went to many parties with Issa's sister and her high-profile police officer friend. One day I bumped into him whilst I was in town. He approached me and asked if I wanted a lift back. He was going to buy some food and invited me to join him. I thought it would be fine as I knew him from the parties with Naema. I felt I could trust him and, after all, he *was* a high-ranking police officer.

I went to his big American type of car and got into the passenger seat. He drove me with a big smile to Manama, to a flat that was semi-furnished with just a few chairs, table and a bed. I started to feel uncomfortable because he then proceeded to lock the door with a key from the inside. He then laid out all the food and asked me to eat with him, which I did as I was hungry. But all the while I was thinking that he was up to something. Once we finished our food, he literally forced himself on me, I had no choice, the door was locked and he was in a high position with the police. Who could I tell?

He left after he had his way with me. His English was very limited so even a proper conversation was not possible when I started protesting and reminded him that he had a girlfriend already. All he would say to me was 'halawa', meaning beautiful.

He left me in the flat, didn't offer to take me home and locked me inside. I had no way of getting out. The windows all had bars on them. I remember looking out of them and calling out, but the people that lived in those flats wouldn't dare come near me. They were Indians and they were afraid to approach me as they knew who he was. In those days, if you were an Indian you had to cross the road if an Arab was approaching. You couldn't walk on the same side as them.

During the day, I would just stare out the window, watching the Indian people walking by, the children playing nearby. This entertained me during the days I was locked inside. The police officer would come every day with food and drink for me and, as usual, sleep with me. I didn't resist; I knew my life would be in danger if I resisted.

After a few days had passed, I was his prisoner and didn't know what he would do next. He came in to the flat and took out some money from his pocket and told me to go. I headed straight for the bar at the Gulf hotel and drank until I was quite tipsy. Then I proceeded to head home to Naema's.

I didn't dare tell anyone about what had happened. I was so scared of this man's position. After all he was the one taking us to the parties in the Palaces and he knew everyone there. I had to accept my fate and move on.

I decided that I wouldn't stay with the family after that, and by then I already had some new contacts. I decided I would go out on my own and be sponsored by contacts that managed hotels or owned them. I always managed to get a good deal staying at hotels as some were very cheap to stay at, especially if you knew the owner!

There was a hotel in Manama that had an Arabic band playing in one of the big banquet rooms every weekend. I had met one of the drummers previously when I was out at a nightclub and he mentioned he played there, so I went to see his band, on the evenings I had no invitation to a party. The first night I walked into a room filled with only men from Saudi, drinking like no tomorrow, who were staying at the hotel. The band was playing and I liked the music, so I decided to get up and dance. I stayed close to the band.

There was no designated dance floor but staff there allowed me to dance because I knew the drummer from the band. There were times the floor staff had to monitor the intoxicated men wanting to dance with me. It was manageable for them in the beginning to control the odd man coming up to me and trying to dance with me. In return I was offered to eat free from the buffet being served from lunchtime till the band finished. I was satisfied at that deal as I thoroughly enjoyed being there, the live music was great and I was always happy to be dancing.

One evening whilst dancing I noticed the Sheikh, my friend, was there with a group, so I went over and said hello. He introduced me to his friends and I stayed at his table for a drink until I went back to dance. Soon I was receiving garlands of red flowers. I was told they were from the Sheikh. Although they are supposed to represent money, I didn't get any that night. I didn't mind as I was enjoying myself – I thanked the Sheikh for the flowers and he left later to go to another venue.

I went back a few times to eat freely at the buffet, and always got offered drinks by the band or someone there. It was becoming a regular place I went to whenever I was free for the night. The band were always inspired to play better when I arrived. Otherwise it was just playing to men that were more interested in drinking at the bar.

One night I felt I danced especially well. I was very much into the flow of the band and felt I was one with them. I particularly enjoyed dancing to the drum beats. I would move my body to every sound that was played, as though in an orchestra. I became an instrument in movement.

That evening, there was a particular older man who was insisting on dancing with me and wouldn't give in. The security tried many times to get him to sit down, however he was very insistent that he wanted to dance with me. This changed the energy in the place. I had one of my colour aura visions. Suddenly, before my eyes a vibrant red energy appeared. The man had another friend trying to get onto the dance floor as well. The bouncer couldn't control them and was telling them to get off the floor. The next minute another man joined in and started dancing crazy, arms flapping around. The bouncer then called in another man to assist him and that's when a fight broke out, which in turn escalated into a room of men fighting each other. The energy of the room was so pronounced with RED, it was as though I could foresee what was going to happen before it occurred. There were chairs flying across the room, men smashing up the place, it was a mess. The band stopped playing and fled. I was told to leave too. It was disastrous and because of that incident I was told that I couldn't go and dance there anymore.

There were other places where I danced that paid a fee for just turning up and then whatever you made on top of that was yours. This were usually at private parties held by high-ranking government officials and rich business men. Sometimes it was at some Sheikh's garden. You were guaranteed an amount for just attending especially if you were invited to dance. Once you attended, all you needed was to dance a couple of times and you would get something from the host. If you danced a lot more to impress the men in the room, then it was up to you. If I wasn't into the types of people invited, I would just sit back and drink and eat from the prepared dishes that were always served, freshly made and enough to satisfy the most discerning.

There was one particular Arabic club in Manama that I absolutely enjoyed going to. The music was always pumping and filled with rich patrons that would drive in from Saudi Arabia or even from other States like Kuwait. They played the most recent hits and played the music loud. When I arrived with a girlfriend whose name was Baby, we would hit the dance floor for hours! One night I was extremely into the flow of the music and, as it was a crowded night there, was squashed next to an older man at a table with friends that were drinking freely and watching the dancers on the floor.

I was very close to his table and I was still able to move in my limited space with the music surging through me, every movement defined and in perfect timing. I was suddenly one with the music and knew what would happen. The man next to me suddenly pulled out his wallet and emptied all his money on top of my head. The waiters saw what was happening and dived towards me to stop me from collecting the money. I was told that I couldn't have it, even though the man did this out of his acknowledgment of my exceptional dancing that night. I wasn't going to argue about it as I wasn't very confident in speaking out then, so I allowed them to do this. They could have pocketed the money themselves but I didn't argue about it. The older man seemed undeterred by what happened and just wanted me to keep dancing. He did offer my friend and I a drink if we wanted one. He had a big bottle of whiskey on the table that was being shared by the group.

These were the times I did feel that my passion for dancing was my calling. It was such a peaceful, serene, unification with God as I was fully in the moment in Oneness through dance!

I remember one night in Bahrain earning $1,400 – that was the most I ever got dancing. I was so happy. I could pay the rent on my place in London and buy a few luxury items. I was into designer clothes at a young age. I finished at the party and decided to go to one of the large hotels to have a drink. I met some guy at the bar who told me there was a party upstairs, so I followed him up. I had a drink, then woke hours later. My money was gone and there was a strange guy in the bed next to me.

I was about to call the police, when the guy in the bed got on the phone and not long after a big burly man in his early thirties entered the room wearing a white thobe. I noticed that there was a gun in a holster and started to panic at that moment, as I had heard of stories where women disappeared in the Middle East. He immediately started asking me questions – who I was and who I knew?

I told him the name of the Sheikh I knew, from all the parties. His face changed from being serious to breaking out into a smile. He said, "Oh, you know my cousin. You are lucky, your money will be with you in a few hours time." What a relief, I got out of this situation because of who I knew!

I waited in the room for over four hours and finally an envelope arrived with my missing money. I knew I couldn't do much more about the incident because in those days the Sheikhs were the absolute law there. They could do anything and not blink an eye – the people were totally loyal to the Sheikhs.

I did meet a lot of influential people in Bahrain and dated some absolute dream boats. There was one guy I dated a few times who turned out to be the Crown Prince's body-guard. I recall his name being Essa and he invited me to the palace one day, it was a private party held by the Crown Prince in the late 1970s at one of his smaller residences – it was still palatial in size.

I walked in thinking about how great the party would be and what I saw disappointed me. The Crown Prince was sitting on a couch with a few Gulf Air ladies next to him. He invited me to sit but I declined. There was only English music playing and I was so annoyed that no-one there was interested in having a dance and there was no Arabic music to dance to. I was hoping to earn some money dancing!

I had met the Crown Prince previously at my Sheikh friend's office one other time when I needed him to help me out with my overstay there. He just picked up the phone to the authorities and fixed it on the spot. When I went in to Immigration to stamp my passport, the officer in charge was a lot nicer to me after the call from the Sheikh.

He asked me, "Why didn't you tell me you knew the Sheikh?" His face was all bright red with embarrassment that he had yelled at me previously and threatened me with a big fine. It was so handy knowing this Sheikh, he always came through for me and even if he wasn't around. I just mentioned his name and that was enough to get me out of a pickle. I looked at him as my Guardian Angel in those days.

The Crown Prince was head of the BDF when I first met him at the Sheikh's office, he came in with his full uniform. I was sitting opposite the Sheikh telling him about my visa issue when the Prince walked in and they both saluted each other and then I was introduced. You could see there was a lot of respect between them – after all, they were related.

I told Essa (the bodyguard) that I wanted to leave the party as the gathering wasn't lively enough for me, so we drove away in his Mini Moke and as he was driving we encountered a swell of water created from the rains. There were no proper drains at that time in Bahrain – and it is still mainly desert – and when it rained huge parts of the island would be flooded. Essa decided to take a chance and drive through it, and sure enough, the car just sank into the water and we were completely wet from being totally immersed in the water. It was funny in a way, except that I had nice clothes on for the party and they were ruined! He was a lovely guy although his English was almost zilch. We lost contact after I left to go back to London.

I always thoroughly enjoyed my time in Bahrain. After a month I decided to go back to London, but was soon planning to go back to Bahrain again. After all, dancing was my passion and I could get paid for doing it there.

14

London Oil Sheikhs

London was filled with so many Arabic people around the time I was there, during the mid–late seventies. I met so many wealthy rich Arabs during this time, because this was where they were all holidaying at that time. I had heard previously Lebanon was their holiday of choice, however with all the fighting and destruction going on they couldn't go there anymore. Even Egypt was losing popularity with the tourists. All attention was now in London.

The wealthy Sheikhs and businessmen were also buying up big in London. It was a great time to buy properties at low prices. The wages were also low in London then, I remember the nurse telling me she only earned thirty pounds a week.

I always seemed to encounter Arabs from the Gulf wherever I went. I was attracted to their extreme wealth and how generous they were towards me. I did enjoy the attention I was getting from them – after all, they were lovely grounded people too and I did have a connection with Middle Eastern culture. I just loved the food, dancing, music and the lifestyle they lived. I liked how they respected their elders and looked after their family in old age.

I met Mohammed when I was out having fun dancing at a club, he told me he was from Bahrain and staying at a three-star hotel with his friend for a couple of weeks on holiday. He invited me to visit him at his hotel room the next day and we would go out during the day. When I arrived late morning, I noticed his friend had a blow-up doll in the bed with him. I was quite naive about what it was, as I had never seen one before. I had a good look at it wondering why would he have a plastic doll in bed with him.

Mohammed took me out exploring the sights of London that day. He was a real gentleman.

There was a big Sheikh from Dubai arriving with his entourage visiting London, and I was invited to join them. I arrived earlier so I could greet the Sheikh when he arrived at the downstairs foyer at the Intercontinental hotel. I was also approached by an Arab speaking woman working at the hotel, who couldn't understand why I was invited to join the Sheikh's group. I just shrugged my shoulders when she asked. I suppose it was the usual answer: they liked my dancing. Within an hour, there were a dozen people all waiting for the big 'Oil Sheikh' to arrive. When he did arrive, all we did was to follow him around the hotel. Then we walked to the casino nearby, which was in Mayfair.

I was interested in playing the tables to win my rental money, so my focus was on that. I was very naive about how wealthy this Sheikh was – and anyway, he wasn't my type, maybe over forty-five, and that was too old for me. I was almost twenty then. My attention went onto the blackjack table, the Sheikh noticed how my eyes were on the tables and threw a chip towards me. It was for twenty-five pounds, and with that I played a few rounds to win my rent for the month, which was over sixty pounds. I was elated but unfortunately no-one waited for me. Had I missed out on maybe getting a bigger tip if I had hung around longer? The missed opportunities!

I got by on my looks and my passion for dancing, so I never thought about a career. I was dating so many different men. Some were English guys, one was an actor on TV. I wasn't settled enough to be with one guy – after all there was so many dating offers. I was confused as to what I wanted out of a man other than having fun then.

My flatmates were English girls from the country and we went out together most nights. I was dancing and meeting guys and getting them to buy a bottle of champagne for us to share or try and get them to invite us for dinner. My friend Dawn had a male friend, an Iranian film director, who invited us to watch him gamble at the Mayfair Casino. I remember watching him play with large amounts – up to as much as five hundred pounds at a time. It was a private room and the game was baccarat. I couldn't believe my eyes when the big chips that looked like gold bars were placed on the table. This man played for a good half hour, and didn't blink an eye at his losses.

My twenty-first birthday was coming up months later and my flatmate said that we should invite the film director for dinner at a plush restaurant, near Victoria, facing the water. I happily agreed and she contacted him to help celebrate my birthday. He was happy to accept and said, that he would come along that night, after he finished with his business meeting.

We arrived at the restaurant and were greeted by the staff wearing togas which showed their bare, toned legs. We were quite amused and dared one another to lift up their skirts. Once

I had consumed a few drinks I was confident enough to ask our waiter whether he wore underwear under his toga. He just smiled and walked off…

The three of us enjoyed the night – eventually. After being seated at the table for a while, waiting for the director to arrive, we decided to order as we were hungry. We chose our meals and then decided on a bottle of Dom Perignon as well, expecting the director to turn up. The waiter brought out the cake after dinner, but our friend still hadn't showed up by then. Once the cake was cut, I gave slices to other diners nearby to celebrate my special day.

When the bill was placed on our table after we delayed paying for as long as possible hoping he would turn up. We soon realised, when we looked at the amount, that we didn't have enough money to cover it. Soon we were saying out aloud, "How can we pay it for it?" while also making comments like, "They may make us wash the dishes, what are they going to do with us?" Before I knew it, the other diners put their hands in their pockets and all contributed to the bill. What a relief! They were so kind and generous; I think it was because I gave them a piece of my birthday cake and understood we were in a pickle with the bill. I assume we were loud enough for the others to know what the problem was.

The next day I got a phone call from the film director, that he was stuck in a meeting and he was so apologetic, he would drop by and reimburse me for that. The bill was as I recall, one hundred and twenty-five pounds. That was quite a lot in those days!

He ended up giving me two hundred pounds so I decided to buy some clothes for myself at one of the best department stores in Knightsbridge the following day. I went to Harvey Nichols to look for a few lovely pieces of clothing. They were exquisite but also very expensive. I tried on many pieces of clothing even though the prices were out of my price range.

The sales lady was very helpful with her attention fully focused on helping me select the jumpers and pants, when a very elegantly dressed woman with dark hair in a bun came over to me to express how much she liked the clothes I tried on. She had been waiting to be served and was watching me come out of the dressing room, trying on many different pieces of clothing. She was dressed in black pants and jacket and looked very smart. She remarked how wonderful I looked in them and I must buy, especially the black pants and red jumper.

I thanked her for her comments and went back to the counter to tell the sales lady I would come back again. She was gasping at what just happened. "Do you know who that was?" I said, "No, who was it?" She replied, "One of the most famous ballet dancers of all time, Margot Fonteyn!" I didn't know of her then, but realised how lucky I was to have met such an amazing ballet dancer, who was by then in her fifties. I started hearing more about her later, I wish I was able to have engaged longer in a conversation with her when she had approached me but I thought I was just speaking with a petite, elegant lady. I later saw a documentary on her life and recognised that it was the woman I had met years earlier!

While back in London I heard news that my friend the Sheikh had just had surgery at a Harley Street clinic. So I contacted him to wish him a quick recovery. He called me back a few days later to invite me to a party at his suite and said I could invite my friends as well.

My friends and I arrived and I was so happy to see the usual Arabic band set up to play. I naturally went straight to the dance area. There were many distinguished men in suits or thobes walking around. I didn't know anyone there except the Sheikh and the band members. My girlfriends talked with the guests and enjoyed the attention. The drinks and conversations were flowing, most men and women were busy getting to know each other – except for me. I just danced and danced to my favourite Arabic band.

Once I finished dancing, the Sheikh came over and gave me a hundred pounds for dancing. I didn't expect that. It was a nice surprise. I thought it was just a party with a few guests and drinks provided. I didn't expect the full band to be flown in from Bahrain to entertain the guests as well.

There was another time I went to the Sheikh's apartment in London and his English girlfriend Fiona was there with some other friends. I was sitting on a cushion on the floor with the others, when in walked an older well-dressed English man who was carrying a rectangle box with him. He opened it and I saw an assortment of jewels – brooches and rings. I wasn't close enough to see the full contents, but I was hoping we could all choose from it. Unfortunately, not so. It was only for Fiona's eyes. She had to pick out one thing from it. I was so envious that she got a real jewel. I found out the man was from Graff – one of the most expensive and renowned jewellers in London.

My two girlfriends made some good contacts from the parties and went on to their own adventures after I left later back home. I didn't have any contact with them until years later. One is living in London and married a lovely Iranian who invested in many properties there.

15

Back to Bahrain

I was still in contact with Mohammed (the guy I met in London) and he invited me to visit in Bahrain to stay at his father's hotel. I didn't realise that he came from a wealthy family that owned many properties there. In particular, they owned a very large hotel with a huge car parking space surrounded by bars and clubs on the property. I remember having dinner with him and his dad at this big table filled with so much food. His father was very pleasant and I was treated very generously by them. It would have been great to have that lifestyle, however I wasn't in love with Mohammed. He was just a passing thing for me. But, he did find the love of his life soon after, I heard.

I stayed at his hotel quite a few times at a discounted rate because of our friendship, and a few years later he met up with me to tell me about his progress in life and how much he loved his wife. He was very dedicated to his religion and I saw how he lit up with light when he spoke about his faith and his wife. He had opened many shops in the Gulf region that produced different types of pastries and also served coffee. He had made himself even wealthier by then.

The cake shop in the hotel complex was always open till very late. I always dropped in every time I stayed there after a night out for a cake and coffee. There was usually someone I knew there, or, if not, then I would end up talking to the customers anyway – that's how friendly the people are.

I stayed at a different hotel during one visit to Bahrain. It was called the Omar Khayyam and I couldn't believe how often the phone rang for me. It seemed like every few minutes the phone was ringing and ringing with men offering to take me out. I remember a well-known member of the Kanoo family invited me for dinner. I had never experienced anything like that before in my life.

I was so overwhelmed by the phone calls and I later found out why this happened. The hotel workers would contact people to tell them about who was staying at the hotel, giving them the room number in return for a generous tip. I was always curious as to who was behind the phone calls but never discovered who it was, as I was already too busy enjoying my time there. I had no shortage of men to date.

I stayed there over a week and was presented with a huge bill before checking out. I hadn't even thought about paying for the room or where the money was coming from – until it happened! I rang around and asked if anyone would help, and luckily Mohammed from the band got the money for me (my guess is from the Sheikh). He paid for the room and checked me into another cheaper room he found. I could have made the money dancing, but it takes a little while to get the invitations.

Whilst in Bahrain in an area called Zallaq, I visited the Ruler's Beach, which was only open to Westerners. I went there hoping that I could meet the Ruler and that he would invite me for afternoon tea, as I knew he did entertain most days. I would usually go there, have a swim, get free refreshments and then wait for his limo to drive up. I would see him go into his beach residence then come outside into his garden area, that was fenced off and guarded, to have afternoon tea with one or two female guests.

He was well regarded for his generosity there, and I heard many stories of how he helped out Westerners that he befriended. He was a bit plump in his earlier years, but towards the end of his reign was very thin and looked so much shorter.

Years later my friend the Sheikh told me about his death when he came to visit Sydney for the Olympic Games. I was in Melbourne and he rang to invite me to come and visit him in Sydney. It was an unexpected call from the Sheikh at that time. He had the receptionist try my number in Sydney first, before they tried Melbourne. The Sheikh spoke to me and invited me to join him in Sydney as he was part of the Olympic Committee. I booked my flight immediately and my girlfriend Jenny came a few days later to join me. I was very ill with a bad flu that I couldn't shake off – it was still lingering after two weeks but that wouldn't stop me seeing my Sheikh friend who I looked up to. I had known him for many years by now and he always said, he enjoyed my dancing.

Whilst in Sydney I wasn't up to doing much except sleeping or drinking and attempting to eat what was on offer. Each evening we all sat together on the floor and lots of dishes were placed onto a tablecloth. The food tasted very bland and I couldn't eat much at all because of the flu bug I had. But I managed to go one day to the athlete's village. I looked around and stayed close to the Sheikh. It was a nice experience to be invited there, although I wasn't well enough to enjoy it as much as I would have liked to. I went and ate at the amazingly big eating area catered for everyone. I was able to choose from many dishes and that was one day I did eat well.

We stayed at a four-star hotel with his entourage of guests. There were pokie machines downstairs in the gaming room, and every day the Sheikh would give me a hundred dollars to gamble. At that time I was in need of a fridge so once I won some money I would put it aside. Every day I managed to win so I ended up with enough money by the end of the week. The only time I lost was on the last day, and that was the only time the Sheikh won.

Before he left Australia, I asked him if he would help me get a passport so I could travel freely to Bahrain. After all, it had become like my second home by then. He offered to sponsor me first, then after deep contemplation agreed. He knew how much I loved his home as I travelled there so many times in the early days when Westerners were a rare sight to see then. I had always bumped into him at some party or venue. It seemed that my timing was uncanny, to connect with him many times whilst I was out dancing somewhere.

The Sheikh was going onto to Thailand after Sydney with his entourage afterwards. When we were leaving, he opened up a large suitcase filled with gifts, perfumes, Dupont pens, and gold jewellery. He took out a large gold chain with a Koran that he placed around my neck and said that it would help protect me, as I wasn't well still. I was very grateful receiving that gift from him, and sure enough I soon recovered quickly after that. He also gave me perfume, which I gave to my neighbour as a gift when I got home.

I was happy to be back home to rest up after that unexpected surprise.

16

Back in London

I had returned to London no richer after Bahrain, as usual. I was always told by the Arabs I met there, that I was the only one that left the island poor and not rich like all the other Westerners that came to visit. Many women went there to catch a wealthy husband or meet a rich Sheikh and live on easy street. I did like the idea of having money but it wasn't enough for me, I wanted love as well. Even though I wasn't sure of what I was looking for then. Following my passion of dancing and the desire to fill that void within – that was a start.

In London I was scraping up money for the rent when it was due. I was really going through a tough time, and the only time I got money was when I danced at parties. I wasn't confident enough to go and get a belly dancing job at the big clubs. I had been to one famous club one night and the women there were from the Middle East and they were very beautiful and voluptuous. I had gone with some gentleman who took me for drinks there, it was an awesome sight to see. Millionaires were handing out thousands of pounds to the dancer. They were stringing notes together to make a very long garland to place over her. I remember wishing I was that beautiful.

I got by mainly due to my dancing and my looks were somewhat attractive, although I never fussed over how I dressed and groomed myself. I know I could have enhanced my assets more! Still, I always had men buy me drinks or invite me for dinners and many times I accepted just to get a meal and then thank them and leave.

I remember I went out one night with a group of friends who were just a broke as I was. They were from Italy and squatting in an abandoned mansion. I had met one of the women at a café and she took me to the house they were all living in. It was huge! There was no electricity but that was okay for them. They had kerosene lamps or candles burning at night. It was quite cold in the house though.

This group of friends came out with me one night to a nightclub, all with no pennies to spare. We were sitting with glasses of water on our table when I decided to get up and have a dance. I really got in the groove of the mood and soon attracted an intoxicated Arabic man onto the dance floor. He came over to me and started jumping up and down and every time he jumped a ten pound note would fly out of his pocket, I would then pick it up and place it in my pocket. This went on for some time, I was loving it!

Eventually one of his friends came onto the dance floor to tell him what was happening, but he didn't care. They didn't ask me for the money back, but the friend made him stop jumping and no more money came out. I danced a little while longer with him and thanked him and left the dance floor to count the money out. It was eighty pounds! I went and bought a round of drinks to celebrate and kept the rest for my food for the week and for my fares. That night was great! Eighty pounds was a good week's wage then.

One day when I had to travel on the tube to meet up with a friend on the other side of town, I realised I didn't have enough money for my fare. I didn't know how I was going to get there. I was looking for a miracle and I did get one! I was at the turnstiles outside the station and found a five pound note – I thanked God for helping me. There have been many times that money has appeared for me to get by. I think of it as the heavens helping me out in time of need. I met a Londoner of African descent who turned out to be a con artist. It was the time I was getting restless being in London and thinking of home. I had met him at the nightclub and he took my home number and said he would call me to go for lunch. I was at that stage thinking about my life and I needed a change. London was starting to become mundane. It was all about drinking and sex – and, of course, dancing!

This guy rang me the next morning and asked me if I wanted to earn some money – all I had to do was go with him in some shops and try on some clothes. He would do the rest. I agreed not knowing what he was going to do, because he said the magic word, MONEY! I needed it at that time.

I borrowed a dress from my flat-mate – I only wore pants then, mainly designer brands. We went first to a jewellery shop and he immediately went to look at the diamond rings on display and I could see he was trying to distract the man serving him. When he had the rings in his clutches, the man wouldn't take his eyes off him and we soon left a few minutes later. He then told me how he would go into a shop and when the attendant was showing him the diamonds and other people entered the shop he would then put one in his mouth without gagging and walk out without anyone the wiser.

I felt a bit intimidated by this guy and wanted to back out when I realised what type of guy he was, but I had to go with him as I was totally broke. Anyway, how could I even get home without a fare?

We went into a few boutiques and he would make out as though we were buying a few dresses as we were getting engaged. This was the story he told the sales staff – he was buying me a new wardrobe of clothes. Then would come into the changing room with me, and as I had many dresses to try on, he would stuff some of them into a bag he brought with him. Then after examining me in them outside the dressing room would say, "Oh, I think they don't look so good on her."

The last place I vividly remembered was a very classy boutique. The dresses were very expensive and he had pliers in his bag to cut the sensor tags off the dresses, I said to myself, *that's it, never again!* I was so scared to do this, but I was scared of him too! We walked out of the store and went to his place to check out his day's work. I saw, that one of the dresses still had a sensor tag on – he hadn't cut the tag off! Luckily the main store sensor wasn't on and didn't pick it up! If it had been working I may have been arrested, even though he had the goods.

Once I calmed down, I waited for the money he promised, but he didn't give me anything, just some stout to drink. My heart sunk after all the hours with him knowing he reaped in hundreds! He said he would give me money the next day, after we went shopping again. But I didn't trust him after what happened and made sure I wasn't around after that day. I never answered the door or his calls! I didn't want to start that type of lifestyle. I learned the hard way!

There was a time in Bahrain, when I started travelling there more often, when I thought that I was going to marry one of the Sheikhs. He was a Prince I met when I was out at a café. He was very handsome, and when he introduced himself I felt a spark of light as I was very attracted to him. I could tell he was soon keen on me too. He would invite me to meet up every night for dinner, this went on for a couple of weeks. I was in la-la-land during this time. I couldn't wait to see my Prince each night.

He told me that his family owned the Ramada hotel and we usually met up there to have romantic evening meals in an outdoor private area. We soon were talking about a life together. I was hoping that this dream wouldn't end. Alas it was too good to be true. The Prince was talking about getting engaged one minute and the next he disappeared out of my life.

I found out that he had been asking around, and someone from a previous party I attended told him that I slept with a guy there. I was very sad that he believed this man as I know myself, this would only have happened if my drink had been spiked. I was very fussy about whom I went to bed with at least and I wouldn't have gone for someone at the party. I remember they just weren't my type. But the damage was done, the Prince soon disappeared from my life. I had believed in my heart he would marry me – it was like a fairytale. I was almost going to be a Princess and now it was gone!

There were a few times I did get into dire situations in London. I met an Egyptian, a school teacher, who drank at Pip's Wine Bar in Mayfair and he invited me to stay with him after we had chatted numerous times at the bar. I needed somewhere to stay until I found another place to share. After being with him for a week, I soon realised that I didn't really fancy him enough and didn't want to form a relationship, so I decided to just leave as soon as possible. I had met the couple downstairs and they seemed like a nice couple, of Jamaican background.

I was downstairs one day when the young man called me into his place. He wanted to speak to me, so I went in thinking his partner was home, however she was at work at the time. He had made up an excuse for me to go into his apartment and once in, he tried to get amorous with me, but I refused his advances. He then pulled out a knife and took it to my throat and said if I didn't sleep with him he would kill me. Naturally I obliged – as I wanted to live. I didn't even go to the police about it. I just wanted to forget it happened. So I left that place that same day whilst the Egyptian was at work and never went back.

Another time I went to a club and was invited back to a house with a few men and one woman. I was very intoxicated and remember one of them pulling off my gold chain and taking it. I wouldn't let him have it. This time I did call the police and they managed to get it back for me and told me to go home. I was so far away and couldn't afford a cab, so I asked them to give me a lift. They refused at first, but it was a dark cold night and once they saw I was walking alone in the dark they decided they would help me.

There was also the time I met someone that worked for the Libyan Government. I was out dancing as usual at one of the clubs. A friendly older man bought me drinks and chatted. Before he left the club, he invited me to his suite at the Intercontinental hotel one afternoon for drinks. I agreed, thinking he was nice to me, a real gentleman. That was so far from the truth, though! I went to see him and he offered me a cocktail, one late afternoon. I remember we were laughing together, then the next thing I knew I was waking up in another room to the sound of men talking to each other in Arabic and a complete stranger having sex with me. I opened my eyes in shock and the man suddenly raising his voice to tell the others I was awake, then suddenly I passed out again.

I don't remember anything more about it, except now I know that my drink was spiked and I was raped by a few men that night.

I was so used to being abused by men by then, I just numbed myself with drinking and pushed that memory down to repress dealing with it. I wasn't strong enough to stand up for myself.

One of the workers at Pip's Wine Bar where I frequented, asked me if I would like to take a trip to Egypt for free, I would stay a week with his family, all food was included as well. The only thing I had to do was just take a suitcase packed with clothes through customs. I thought about it that night and decided there was no risk, after all it was only clothes in the case, and I would accept. He explained that the family had a clothing boutique and the tax on clothes was extremely high in Egypt so at times they would travel back home from London with new clothes to save on taxes.

He booked our tickets for a couple of weeks later, and together we boarded the plane and he took a seat further away from me. He told me that he thought if they saw us together they would search my luggage on arrival so by sitting away from me they wouldn't think I was with him, I was fine with that, I was happy to be going on a trip away, didn't mind the seating arrangements.

The plane landed early in the morning and immediately after collecting my suitcase, I was approached by a customs official who asked what I was doing in Egypt. He also asked who my travelling companion was, and then asked me to open my luggage (which I had never packed or looked at). I obliged and inside were brand new clothes in packaging. Nothing at all had been worn. The officer then questioned me about the new clothing, and as it was close to Christmas I replied that they were gifts for people I knew here. Well as he didn't know what to say to that, he agreed that I could take out what I could carry out with me as there were far too many new clothes and there were could be high taxes on them. I agreed and just took an armful and trotted off towards the exit happy to be finally in Egypt.

The guy wasn't very pleased at what I had done. When I exited the customs area, he complained that I could have taken a lot more of the clothes with me. He had to find a way to pay someone in customs for the rest of the clothes they confiscated. I wasn't concerned about that, though, and after I had met his family, I left my bag at their house and took off to explore the city.

After changing my money I asked some locals how to get around to the tourist sites. I was told to take a bus. I managed to visit some famous sites, then decided to walk around the market. By late afternoon I came across a beautiful looking hotel amongst the decay and old buildings in Cairo. It was a five-star opulent hotel facing the Nile. I walked into the foyer in awe of its size and beauty. Walking around I noticed I had caught the attention of some guy at a nearby bar. Once eye contact was achieved, he then quickly walked over to me and asked where I was from, and if I'd like a drink with him. I ended up spending a lovely afternoon chatting and laughing with him; he turned out to be a nice guy. He told me he was visiting Egypt from another Middle Eastern region and staying at the hotel on a business trip.

As the afternoon wore on, he asked if I would like to have dinner with him in his suite. I felt safe with him by then, so agreed. He called room service and ordered a sumptuous spread. I remember it was a fillet steak with an array of vegetables to choose from. I started eating when my stomach started growling. I had to suddenly get up and run to the toilet. I then realised I had diarrhoea bad! I couldn't move out of the toilet the whole night. I stayed put. Every time I tried to get up and walk towards the door I had to rush back on the toilet. I decided I just had to stay there, with the date knocking on the door intermittently for hours, asking me to come out.

The guy gave up on me after time and went to bed. He tried his best to coax me out of the bathroom. He knew it was futile after many hours, so he went to sleep.

My symptoms eased by the middle of the night. I was so drained from the whole saga. I decided to lie down on the couch so I wouldn't disturb the man for the few hours left before morning. I was greeted very early by the guy looking very disappointed at the outcome for him. He had to check-out and get to the airport, so there was no time to meet up again. He put me in a cab to the home of the family I was staying with and said goodbye. (Lucky for me, I had asked the sister to write down their address).

On my return, I was greeted by the sister who had told me they had been looking for me part of the night when I didn't come back by the evening. I apologised and told them what transpired. She said that I had a glass of water with ice in it at their place before I left and maybe it was the ice, as that was obtained from the tap water to make up the ice cubes. It didn't affect them though, as they had built up a tolerance to the water there.

My stomach settled after that, although I was very cautious as to what I ate and drank after that. I stayed a few days more days in the family home, then went back to London earlier than planned, as the guy was really annoyed that I didn't take more clothes out of the suitcase at the airport.

He came back with me and went his way, no gratitude that I even tried and agreed to do this for him – after all, I was the one that was taking the risk. In hindsight, I realised that the luggage could have contained more than just the new clothes and I could have been put in jail. How immature and reckless I was to do that! But it turned out okay anyway, as I did get to Egypt and see the pyramids at least on that first day.

With everything that happened, I decided enough was enough. I wanted to go home back to Australia, so I rang my mum to get me a ticket back to Melbourne. She paid for my ticket immediately, so I was ready to leave, en route to Bahrain for one last time for a few days before going home to Australia. Bahrain was just a short trip, so I couldn't get anything happening there. It's like slow motion there as the weather is so hot in the summer months, and everything is at a snail's pace.

Leaving Bahrain for the last time – knowing it would be a long time before I returned – was a mixture of emotions. I was leaving a place which I regarded as my second home. The feeling I had when I was there was as though my soul felt at ease and was at home – even though I had Greek background. Perhaps in my last lifetime I was from the Gulf region? I always felt that I was a long lost Soul – a princess who was trying to find her way home. I tried my best to find happiness, but never was able to hold onto it.

17

Back Home

I arrived back in Melbourne and stayed at my parent's former home in Fitzroy. They had moved to their new house and allowed my sister and I to rent out the house before they eventually sold it. It felt a relief to be home safe, but also quite boring compared to where I had been, on many adventures and challenges. I was still quite unsettled and needed to get my feet back on the ground after almost two years away.

I went visiting my friend, a neighbour, a few days later as I was now in need of money and I knew my girlfriend would offer to buy some of the items that I brought over to show her. I agreed to sell her my beautiful peasant style designer top made by Yves Saint Laurent (it was my new favourite piece and hardly worn) and my gold 18ct rings that were gifts. I did have some beautiful pieces of designer clothing, however my friend who was short and a few pounds overweight wasn't able to get into any of my pants or fit into shoes. I was super slim by the time I arrived back home.

I was soon thinking of getting a job after a few weeks back – there was only one thing I was good at and adored, which was dance, and that was all I could do at that time. There weren't many opportunities in dance though at that time in Australia.

I dated a few men whilst being back, nothing serious, until one day my neighbour Danny brought over his friend in his sports Mercedes. He looked like the mafia types I had seen on the television. I was intrigued to know more about him, so I inquired after who he was. Danny told me the next day that his friend, called Mario, had asked after me as well. So he planned for us to meet at the Bombay Rock club for drinks on the coming Friday night.

I remember that night of our first date that Mario was constantly buying me drinks – up to a dozen vodka and oranges that night – and also that he was super shy. We decided to go for a coffee after the club closed and instead of putting sugar in his hot chocolate, he accidentally put in salt and still drank it! That's how shy he was then!

The night went smoothly and he dropped me off at home and asked me if I'd like to watch his horse race the next day. In the morning he rang to arrange to pick me up and that was when I could see how besotted he was with me, that he was doing whatever he could to be in my life. He was obsessed with me and would not leave my side and did everything he could to entice me into becoming his partner.

When he took me to the racetrack the following day, I saw him bet on his race horse, who already had a few city wins and was a favourite at Flemington that day. He put a thousand dollars on it to win. I looked through the race form for the first time and told him I liked another horse – my intuition told me to pick that one, so I put five dollars each way on it. Guess what? Mine won at thirty-three to one! Mario would have won a fortune if he backed it. I remember I just loved the name of it – Halim Pasha – and had mentioned to Mario before the race how much I really liked the horse.

I had many wins on the horses over a period of a few months, winning on long shots most of the time too. During that time, I was taking driving lessons and tipping the instructor each week and my horse tips always won! He was always stumped how I picked the winners. He also told some of his friends after a few weeks of my winning and they won a small fortune too! It was just beginner's luck. It didn't last for too long – just a few months. Mario bought some horse shares soon after and was getting good wins out of them. He had very good city wins from at least three horses and I even bet on them myself.

We were good together, and money started to flow easily into our lives. It seemed that our partnership worked well. He had a small record shop in Footscray and it wasn't making much money when I first met him. His sister worked there and one day she got offered a job at a real estate agency doing admin work, so he asked if I would work there. I had just became pregnant with our daughter and I agreed to work until after her birth.

I had the record company reps come in and at that time there were many up-and-coming artists. Blondie was one singer that really took off. I remember the rep convincing me to buy up big as it was popular and sure to be a hit album. Well, it seemed that I had the knack, as every record I ordered big quantities of sold well and Mario was actually starting to become interested in the business; it was making money rather than losing money. He eventually took over running it and moved around the corner to Irving Street into larger premises where he added imports. This was very timely as he started to build up a reputation as having rare and imported records and began to post them out Australia-wide.

We also added Fred Perry tops and the famous Doc Martens to the list of it. I remember travelling overseas somewhere out of London especially to put in an order and going to the Fred Perry showroom. It was my first time ordering clothes and I thoroughly enjoyed it. We started going so well with these clothing lines, and to this day those names are still popular worldwide.

We were hiring movies and, as it was so expensive in those days, Mario decided that he would start renting out videos himself. He opened up accounts with all the companies, rented out the shop next door to the record shop, and we were booming! Every weekend we had a mile of people lining up to hire out movies at six dollars a pop. We did lose a lot of videos as our filing system wasn't well prepared then and asking for identification wasn't a priority at first, especially if we knew them as regular customers. There were many of them and they gave out their passwords to family members, or other customers overheard the passwords then would use it and take off with the videos. From each loss, we gradually tidied up our rental system.

We moved the record shop to the mall eventually, as it was a much bigger place. We had the clothing stored upstairs. It was my idea to offer customers a one-dollar discount if they were unemployed or pensioners. This really took off as no-one in those days offered a discount on their products. After we had been in the mall a while, we noticed directly opposite us another store opening that offered CDs (as the records were phasing out then). It was Target and they were discounting their CDs in competition with us. This started to affect our sales. However, I thought of placing Crystals and Native American products as well. These really took off and I was getting so many clients coming in to the store just for these products.

Mario had opened up many video shops around that time and our business was booming. We also had a shop in Thomastown that was formerly a huge warehouse. He had space available so he put in the crystals and necklaces. Many of these were made from rose quartz crystals. They were a very popular item in those days as it was a new trend. I had placed some in the Footscray shop with the American Indian items and it took off in such a big way that we just had to place it in the Thomastown store! He also added sports cards and had special staff handling that side of sales. We had so many things going at once.

Mario later opened up a place called Pockets in Bay Street, Port Melbourne, a huge warehouse with fifty pool tables, huge paintings of famous people depicted playing pool or pool balls placed within the painting. We had, in total, four men in the partnership (two were well-known footballers.) It was an amazing place. I was put in charge of hiring the bands and we had them playing Thursday to Sunday.

Our weekends were the best, pulling in the crowds to come play pool, listen to a band, drink and eat. What more would you want for entertainment? I made sure I looked after the regulars and big groups we booked in the evenings. I always threw in a drink or two for them.

My partner brought in a couch one day for extra seating in the warehouse. I loved it and started buying more. I went to a great op shop in my local area that had old 'as new' couches. I placed them around the place, giving it a comfy look. It took off and we had more and more people dropping in and staying longer. I would have to say that this started the trend in all the cafes and clubs after that.

I had a couple of life-changing experiences while I was in a relationship with Mario. There was a time that we went to Sydney for a holiday and also for a big race meeting. Mario always wanted to get to the racetrack on arrival and would leave me at the hotel if I didn't want to go along. This particular day I was feeling anxious and very confused about my life. I wasn't very happy with myself and searching still. I had a good lifestyle, but I felt a void in me that I needed to fill somehow.

I went to the front of the hotel that faced the beach and decided to lie down on the sand. I was feeling tired and drained, like I was sinking into the sand, when suddenly a strange feeling came over me – energy was spiralling up my body, shooting up towards my crown area. In a flash, I saw my soul come out and float high above me. I observed myself as a soul with a fine cord attached to my lifeless body on the sand. The cord was a translucent colour and I was aware of the body on the sand appearing like the carcass of a slaughtered animal. No life or energy came from it. It was a dark sight. A message came to me, telling me not to sever the cord. If I did, I wouldn't be able to get back into my body.

I would die!

Moments later I heard a loud chattering, like a flock of birds – like blackbirds or crows – and then my soul jumped back into my body! I started to move and was able to rise into a sitting position. What I saw then were two women talking to each other, sitting right next to me … it could have been them who brought me back into my body again. This was something I would never forget and this was my first experience and proof that the soul did exist.

There was also an incident when Mario and I had the pool hall business and I worked there when we were short of staff at nights. There was a particular time when there were some discrepancies with money missing and lots of alcohol wasn't accounted for in sales. I decided to step in and watch the staff at work. Sure enough, one guy working for us was handing out drinks without receiving payment. It wasn't just this guy that was doing it; some others were doing the same. I can understand it happening given nobody was supervising.

After I caught one particular person giving out drinks, I pulled him up for it, and decided that I was going to work on the same nights he did,.It started getting uncomfortable. One night, I went home and a couple of hours later I was awakened in bed by an excruciating pain in my chest area. I felt as though an entity was moving up my torso and crushing the life out of me. Slowly, it moved, pinning me down with a force. I couldn't move or speak – nothing! I thought that this was it and as the force was moving upwards. This entity felt like it was sitting on my whole chest area. I thought I was going to die.

Suddenly, I thought to look within to find a way out. When I was twenty-seven, I'd started to learn Buddhist practices. Now, I try to say a powerful Buddhist mantra by Avalokitesvara that I used for protection, but no sound came out. I was totally paralysed, so I decided to say it in my mind. I kept repeating the mantra until whatever was crushing me started to move away and soon was lifting off me. Once I stopped reciting the manta, it came back and started crushing me. I immediately knew I had to keep saying the mantra again and as swiftly as possible.

This time I found I had regained my voice so I screamed out the mantra as loudly as I could! When this happened the entity vanished. I was able to recover from the ordeal quickly, although I felt very tired after what had just happened.

But then I developed a strong sense that was something was in the corner of the room, watching me. It was dark, but given the outline of the figure, I could identify it was the guy from work I was having problems with. I knew then that he had something to do with what happened. I had heard that he dabbled in the black arts. I thought it was only gossip, but now I wondered if there could have been some truth to it.

Given I had cleared the dark energy from the room, I knew I was safe and fell into a deep sleep. The next evening when I went in to work, he had given his resignation. How coincidental was that? I felt that I had conquered an evil force that night and moved it out of my life with the help of my Buddhist Mantra.

From that experience, I now think that being in a vulnerable state opens the gates for negative energies to visit.

I now know I was depressed and suffering from anxiety at that time as well, so as a result I was more vulnerable.

18

Martial Arts and Buddhism

At face value, everything seemed okay with my life. However, I still felt very lost and empty within. I had a family, a home, businesses and money, yet something was still missing. I needed to search further for it.

Driving to our shop, most days I'd drive past a dojo and would think I should go in and inquire. Something was pulling me to it, even though all I knew about it was that it was a martial arts training place.

One day, after many months of driving past the dojo, I decided I would knock on the door to inquire about the classes on offer. A few moments later, an older Indigenous lady answered the door. When I asked her about the classes, she smiled at me and told me she would go and get the Dojo Master. Shortly afterward, a man in a dark blue outfit reminiscent of Asian dress greeted me. He looked like a Buddha, bald, clean-shaven and charismatic. He had a sneaky giggle when he laughed, but he was very charming when he spoke. I was intrigued by him, so decided I would try out a class. I told my girlfriend at the time and she was happy to accompany me. We both went the following evening to try it out.

During that first class, the Dojo Master demonstrated how to get out of a neck lock before pinning me down. After many attempts, I eventually managed to break free – although my neck was sore for days after. I was ready to quit after that night; however, my friend really liked being there. There was a guy she fancied there, so I agreed to go back. We became very dedicated students and went at least four nights a week for a whole year.

The following year, the training became harder and the black belts got a bit more serious with us. Some days I was injured by the throws. At times I would be bleeding or have bad mat burns from landing so heavily. My girlfriend decided to leave then. The other lady who was training also left, and I was the only woman still training. I lasted only a short time after that.

Before we started the class, everyone would burn incense to pay homage to the Buddhist icons placed around the room. I was very drawn to this and asked the Dojo Master about it – I wanted to know more.

Six months into the training, the master called me upstairs to his private prayer room. He showed me the four-tiered altar he had built himself and described the ritual items on it. He was laughing cheekily, so I knew something was up. He told me he wanted to "jump my bones". I had never heard the expression before, so I kept quiet.

He then said he was going to take me to meet his Buddhist teacher, as I was inquiring so much into practising this religion, or "philosophy of life" as others describe it.

My Dojo Master was dedicated to many hours of meditation each day. He told me he spent eight hours meditating daily. I was drawn to his energy and wanted to be around him as much as possible. This was the start of an affair. I saw it as a way of connecting to his spirit; he absolutely mesmerised me.

I saw how powerful he was one day when he demonstrated his somersaults to his students – he cartwheeled across the floor and I could see the energy moving along with him! He was a lethal weapon – strong, fit, and running a successful dojo. His students were devoted to him.

The following week we went to see his Buddhist teacher, who had been living in a temple in Asia for over twenty years before he came to Australia. He was of Chinese origin and had lived in a temple in the Philippines, studying Tantra within the Nyingmapa sect of Tibetan Buddhism. When I first met him, he was in his early forties, of medium height and solid frame. His English was slow and unclear; however, by listening attentively, I understood his instructions. Many times he called me to give him a lift wherever he needed to go, and I obliged, even though I wasn't keen on driving to unfamiliar places. He lived miles away from me, but I saw it as a service to my teacher.

On the evening I met my new teacher, I felt his gaze go right through to my soul. I felt a stirring within me and averted my eyes, noticing black stripes painted on the white wall. It looked like the stripes were moving up across the ceiling. I started feeling strange – almost as if I'd taken LSD. I looked back at the teacher and I saw his head detach from his body. It was like a weird dream. I wasn't frightened – *it's just an aspect of what he is capable of,* I thought. Moments later the vision left and I came down from my elevated high.

The teacher, Mr So, took out a small book about the Buddha's life and asked me to take it home, read it, and start on the Refuge Mantra. He instructed me to recite it 100,000 times before coming back to him. I was so excited to start on my new path with Buddhist meditation. I was getting closer to my dojo teacher, and we were spending lots of time together without caring how it affected both our families. I was so besotted by him and also yearning to commit to my spiritual practice, that he had a stronghold on me. I didn't feel I was to blame for his marital problems – it turned out he was seeing another female student and had been since before we met, and there had been others before, too.

We were in his meditation room one day, chatting about Buddhism, when his wife came upstairs. The door was open and I distinctly saw a black cloud following her. I was so surprised by what I saw. When someone says a black cloud is hanging over them, it's not just a saying but actually a real manifestation – it's true! I was starting to see more manifestations. My focus was developing and I was going deeper into my inner world. But I had never experienced that particular manifestation before – a black cloud following a person inside a house!

During this time, my Dojo Master built me a four-tiered Buddhist altar in a small back room in our family home. It was a big job, but my commitment to saying the mantras was enough for him to want to do this for me. He covered it in yellow cloth and placed offerings of bowls of flour, water, and rice on the top shelf. This altar became my place of daily devotion. After finishing my mantras for the day, I would take those offerings outside to the flowerbed my master had built, where he had planted chrysanthemums. There, I would pour the offerings for the "hungry ghosts" each evening, which I was instructed to do by my Dojo Master.

One night, I was facing the kitchen window washing the dishes when I noticed a flash of energy zipping back and forward to the flower bed. I looked harder and saw it was a hungry ghost – an outline of energy shimmering into the shape of an entity of some sort. It was nondescript, but I knew it was not of this world. I rubbed my eyes in amazement. It was acknowledgement that indeed there were hungry ghosts taking the offerings.

My enthusiasm for Buddhism was helping me towards healing a void – it was my main focus now. I meditated three hours a day, every day of the week. I was eager to finish off my mantras so I could go back and get new mantras to recite from Mr So. I wanted to catch up to my Dojo Master's level and I dedicated my first seven years to that amount of meditation. After that period, I started to do a lot less, as I was exploring other modalities in healing. I tried out anything new that would enhance my personal growth.

My Buddhist teacher gave me one particular mantra to focus on: Amitayus. The deity represented a long life in this form and boundless energy as Amitabha. One night, my Buddhist teacher Mr So had a vision – the Gods came down to present him a name to give to me. I felt very honoured to receive it from him as I was the only one in the group to receive a spiritual name – Ameriti Mane.

I asked him why he wasn't giving me the more esoteric Buddhist mantras to recite like my Dojo Master. He was far more advanced with the Vajrayana teaching, which was the highest-level and involved Tantra and powerful initiations. Mr So used an analogy to explain why I was on the Mahayana path: "There are many wells and if you are digging at all of them you will never reach the bottom of it to find the water. By digging at just one well, you will reach the bottom and thus find the reward for staying on that one path, which is enlightenment."

After he put it in this perspective, I was satisfied with what I was doing in my practice and have continued with these mantras as part of my life. I also have some others I use when I need them.

19

Six Weeks of Bliss – Enlightenment

One afternoon, after a few months of seeing my martial arts teacher and being on my new spiritual path, he called me to say that he was bringing a friend over to my place. From there, we were going to visit my girlfriend Simone at her home. She died a few years later after being diagnosed with breast cancer, and the toll of the treatments was too much for her to fight. I remember visiting her before she passed away and, when she answered the door, I saw the vision of death following her. By then her energy was all but gone. I was afraid to go into her house, as the energy was so uninviting. It was a short visit.

We all had a drink together before my teacher and I went into her spare room for some privacy. We were embracing passionately, fully clothed on the carpeted floor, kissing and totally surrendering to the moment, absorbed in rapture, when suddenly I felt something happening within me. I saw my Soul moving out of my body, shimmering with energy, as I was lying on top of him. A moment passed, then I witnessed his Soul also starting to move out of his body towards mine. They were moving energetically together and then in an instant both Souls fused into one!

The next moment, I was standing upright, fully energised, radiant in a blissful enlightened state. I was no longer the same person – I was without an ego. Energy coursed through me. I felt at peace and filled with an overwhelming sensation of love!

My partner got up, overwhelmed by what had happened. Although noting his experience wasn't like mine, he had, however, experienced something like never before. He revealed later that he felt as though he'd completed millions of mantras and was high and elated – although nothing as enriching as my own experience.

It seemed that this experience was the ultimate extinction of the ego. I didn't want to continue with my affair with him on the same level as before. I was so fully immersed in love that I didn't need to show affection outwards – I was complete. I would be walking down the street followed by energy that was so vast that it was beyond description. It was pure light – I was like a magnet. People kept bumping into me. I would be walking along a path with lots of room to move and people would head straight into my path towards me because of my strong energy.

I would wake up early in the morning singing with the birds outside my window. They would chirp whilst I was singing and doing my usual chores. I never gotten up that early in my life before – ever!

At the time, we had a business with partners, and a woman that I never saw eye-to-eye with suddenly became my best friend. She invited me over to her house most days for a meal and to be in my presence. I think she was very religious and was moved by what she saw in me.

As I was in this heightened state, I wasn't thinking or questioning anything. I was just fully present and thinking from a higher consciousness, not from the ego at all! Every moment I was fully immersed in a golden light. There were times I would lie on my bed with violet rays shooting out of my head from my Crown Chakra towards the ceiling for hours until I fell into a deep slumber. I wasn't prepared for anything that occurred as I had no control over my thoughts – I was fully present. I had no fear, as I was love in its purest form.

The experience began so suddenly and stayed with me for around six weeks, enriching every pore of my physical body and soul. In that enlightening, unforgettable period, I had other students from the dojo come to visit and sit with me for hours, just to be in my presence. It was a life-changing time and the experience has stayed with me ever since. It has kept me on the path of self-discovery, of learning more and more about myself and also confirming that we are souls in a physical body.

Martial arts students at my place for a party

It left me as suddenly as it began and taught me so much about the truth of who we really are.

People talk and write about being spiritual and their spiritual beliefs, yet few of them have actually had a fully realised experience, or if they have, it's only a glimpse of it. I feel no one has fully captured the experience I had in those weeks in a way that made me feel they had the same connection I had. I imagine there are people out there, but I haven't met them yet.

I wanted to share this with others – to know that it is possible to live in a higher state in your physical body.

20

Dance and Movement Training

During my long-term relationship with Mario, I started taking lots of dance classes with well-known teachers of that era. One of my teachers was Mr Turnball from the Victorian College of the Arts. I had done some classical training first, then decided to focus more on modern ballet. Mr Turnball's classes were held in a building in Nicholson Street, Fitzroy. Later on, I trained with Mr Dowd in the city, learning jazz dance. There were a few other teachers but these two were my favourites and I felt my dance moves were raised to a different level by attending their classes.

My main interest was to enhance my dance skills, but I also become interested in acting. I saw a brochure about a teacher from NIDA school coming to Melbourne to teach a week-long workshop for teachers and professionals in movement skills. I was curious so I went along, mainly to experience a taste of training from one of the best movement teachers in Australia – Keith Bain. He had many dance and movement qualifications and was a delegate for the International Theatre, going to many dance competitions as a judge and setting up several organisations in the dance field. I thought perhaps if I liked the workshop, I might do further study in drama.

I remember how Keith Bain looked – in his mid-to-late sixties, grey-balding head of hair, dressed in a shirt and slacks. He had a very strong presence; he always had his eye on you. He was very aware of his surroundings and whenever I looked up, I would see him looking straight at me with piercing eyes. I couldn't hide anything from him. I felt he was always watching me.

During the week, I attended the classes and was challenged with many scenarios, but managed to get through them without it being noticed that I was a novice. Most of the people attending were experienced drama teachers, so I was pleased to be working up to the required level. There was a day, though, that we were told to do a square dance routine. He showed us the steps and we were all were put into small allocated groups and had to dance to the music in time. Well, after a few times doing it, I lost momentum and looked at someone else to regain my footing. He came over and spoke to me loud enough for everyone to hear, saying, "Why are you watching them? You are much better than that!" I was surprised that he said that in front of everyone, but just blushed and continued on, thinking, *Wow, he likes how I move.*

There was only one more day to go, and by this stage I was getting a bit tired of going. I decided I would leave at lunchtime on the final day. It had been such a long week of training and I was looking forward to finishing earlier. I arrived at class in the morning and was waiting for lunchtime to be announced so I could leave. Time seemed to go very slowly that day and I was wondering when we would stop for lunch. Finally, one of the others got his attention. "It's already past one-thirty. Are we having lunch?" she asked.

He looked down at his watch and couldn't believe it – his faithful watch (which had never let him down) had suddenly stopped. He'd had it for thirty years, he told us, and this was the first time it had ever happened! I even recall seeing his watch – it looked very old, the face was faded silver and the band was a stretchy silver band. I couldn't believe it was almost time to go home. Because there was only just over an hour to go after lunch, I decided to stay on.

We finished at four and everyone said their goodbyes. I went in to thank him for the lovely but challenging week. I didn't expect him to say what he said to me in such a serious tone, expressing that I should be going into the field. He didn't know what to recommend to me – he was from Sydney – so he just wanted to tell me that I should follow through with dance and movement, as I had talent.

I couldn't believe a man of his position would notice me. I wasn't working like everyone else there – they were all professionals. I was just learning more skills. Once I left for home, I thought a lot about what he had said. I believe his watch stopped because if it didn't, I wouldn't have gone to say goodbye in the office and heard that. His words inspired me to go and look for a course in the field of movement and dance.

Eventually I found an advertised course that would be held at Melbourne University, and I applied as a mature-aged student. I attended an interview and felt it went well – the woman interviewing me sensed my passion and I saw a shift happen. This was an indication that I would be accepted.

I got notified the following week that I wasn't accepted and was disappointed. However, a few days later I got a call telling me I was now accepted as someone had dropped out. I was also informed that they were accepting me mainly due to my former dance training and could see that I was very eager to do the course. This was great – my intuition was right!

I started the course soon after, part-time for two years. It had a very demanding workload and in those two years many students dropped out, including my newest friend who dropped out the first year.

At the graduation, there were thirteen of us left out of thirty who were enrolled from the beginning. Receiving a Graduate of Movement and Dance from members of the faculty was one of the most exciting moments of my life. Wearing my gown and academic cap, I was called up and about to collect my award certificate from the head of the department, when she whispered clearly and softly, "I can't believe you made it!" She looked stunned to see that I had been able to complete the course when so many others had given up. I was pleased with myself; movement and dance officially became my area of expertise.

I always think of Keith Bain as someone who came into my life to point out that I am capable of being able to achieve this. I did teach a few classes later, though gave up after a while. I had too many things going on at that time. I have always preferred performing to teaching. When the right opportunity for teaching does happen, it will have to be done my way and will be guided by what my heart directs me to do. I dance an inner dance first, and while the training I received gives me the structure to go with it, I know the Soul directs me to the core of my own dance and I'm able to touch others through it. With my new training, I could explore dance on many more levels.

21

Swami

After my six-week enlightenment experience, I started to feel more content and back to Earth. But I still had a thirst for more. When I ran into my former Dojo Master (we were no longer together after my enlightenment experience – I knew I didn't need him to fulfil my inner needs), he mentioned people had told him about a Hindu guru in a beachside suburb. Because he had been affected by his experience with me, he wanted to explore Tantra more. He was curious to know more about the guru, but was too busy with his dojo, so asked me if I would go and check out the place and let him know what I thought. He trusted my intuition and wanted to know if the guru was as enlightened as his followers claimed.

I was very curious to meet this guru, so I agreed to go the following week. I went to his residence in a beachside suburb and was greeted at the door by a tall thin male with a strange energy, which gave me mixed feelings. I saw him as the Gate Master as he was the one who always opened the door each time I went.

I entered the house and he asked me to follow him into the lounge area to wait until I was called in for meditation with the group of dedicated followers. In the meantime, he asked me if I wanted a glass of water. I said yes – only to remember my mother telling me to be careful when offered drinks anywhere. I remember him coming back with the water and I drank a sip and a moment later, I felt a rush of energy stir within me, so I decided to pour the rest of the water into the plant next to me.

Later, when the guru was about to start the meditation and talk, I went into the main room. I was anxious by then and in a heightened state, but there were many others there and I enjoyed the night. Swami had a lovely presence. He reminded me of the guru Bhagwan Osho. Once meditation ended, we went into the dining area to be served a beautiful Indian meal. I met some lovely people, chatted until after midnight, then drove home.

That night, all my dreams were filled with snakes! I was writhing in bed, very restless. But even though my night was filled with snakes, I still wanted to experience Swami's presence again. I went back the following week, and after sitting down in the lounge area I noticed the plant where I had poured the rest of the water was dead! I didn't know what to think of this – I decided it was just a strange coincidence and kept going back. I thoroughly enjoyed the meditations, music, and food, so I started taking my friends there for an evening out.

I became comfortable with the people going there and one night a couple there were questioning the authenticity of the guru. I mentioned what happened with the plant when I first went there and after that they never came back. That didn't sway me from going, however, and I became a regular until the Swami moved out into the country. After that, I went to his new place every month. It was a lot further away and I wasn't a keen driver. I also went with friends and it was a good social get-together with food and beverages – alcohol was served too, if you wanted it!

I had some memorable experiences during meditation. One night, I felt like my brain was sparking up. I smelled smoke, then afterwards it felt like a cool liquid was running through my brain. I enjoyed all the new experiences. Another time, I was sitting on the floor in a lotus position during the meditation, and as the beautiful Indian music played I felt energy trying to shoot up my spine. It was like energy was trying to move up and through each vertebra, but there were blocks it had to unravel. It was quite uncomfortable for a while, but the pressure eventually eased off and I was fully immersed in the presence of the moment. I wasn't afraid of the unknown – after all, I had experienced enlightenment!

Another time, I took the Swami a poster of one of the Buddhist deities as a gift. It was a summer's day and I was sitting opposite him crossed-legged, enjoying the deep meditative state, when I felt myself levitate slightly. I saw the Swami acknowledge what had just happened. He smiled and went back to his meditative state. We were both enraptured with bliss in the moments that passed. The next time I went there, he was telling everyone he had a new guru and I kept thinking – does he mean me? But he asked me to order many posters of Buddhist deities to hang around all his walls after that experience.

Going there, I noticed my visualisation skills improved and I could close my eyes and picture anything clearly and precisely. It was a lovely experience. I still get notifications of celebrations there – although I now go only once in a blue moon. He lives too far out for me to visit often, even though my heart has a special spot for his ashram due to the experiences I had there.

22

Mary from Bahrain

I started going back to Bahrain when my relationship with Mario was ending in the mid-1990s. I usually stayed at my friend's hotel and went dancing at the nightclub in the hotel grounds. The area was surrounded by bars, so it was a one-stop place for entertainment and accommodation. Arabs, coming from mainly from Saudi, would stay there for the weekend, as it was centrally located and popular. My friend and his family owned it all!

A causeway was built from Saudi to Bahrain so the men could drive to Bahrain for the weekend to let loose. One day I saw them all travelling into Bahrain like they were on a mission. It reminded me of animals let loose out of their cages. Here they were free to do as they pleased, with no restrictions placed on them. In Saudi, no drinking is allowed and women are covered up. The causeway would be jam-packed with the thousands crossing into Bahrain for the weekend. It was a sight to see.

I was on the highway once, being driven by a male friend, and watched men streaming along the causeway – a single woman's delight if she wanted to meet a man in Bahrain on the weekend. I would say that your chances of meeting a man are much higher there than anywhere else in the world. Not just that, a lot of the Gulf men are quite handsome, in particular those that are educated and know how to conduct themselves with the opposite sex. I met many of them while out dancing.

I also spoke to taxi drivers who told me about the women that were brought into Bahrain covered up. They travelled with a relative as an escort and, once there, took off their *abayas* and wore revealing dresses to go off to the Arabic clubs, drinking and mixing with the men – which is not allowed and punishable in Saudi.

Mary, a Bahraini, spoke English fluently. She was a small-framed, short, plain-looking woman in her fifties who saw me dancing at the night club I frequented. She approached me to ask if I would dance with a man sitting with her. She introduced me to her brother who, she added, was shy and wanted to meet me. I happily danced with him for a couple of tunes and went to the table to chat with him later while he ordered us drinks. After a few minutes chatting, he admitted to me that he was just her friend. That was the first time I met her and already could see she was a liar. I excused myself and went back to dancing on my own. I knew everyone there and felt comfortable going in alone. Anyway, my room in the hotel was only metres away.

A few months later, when I had gone back to Bahrain again from London, I found a different club close to the hotel and decided to check it out. There I met a young woman who was African-American. She had left the navy and decided to stay on in Bahrain. She loved dancing and after dancing near me with her older friend, she decided to approach me and introduce herself. Her name was Baby, and we ended up dancing together. We were a great pair on the dance floor. Her friend wasn't so interested in dancing so she sat at the table chatting to men she had met there.

Baby and I became friends after that night and went out dancing together every weekend – what fun we had! After a couple of weeks, she told me she had a spare room at her apartment and invited me to move in with her. This was great and so much cheaper than staying at the hotel. I could see the opportunities available to those living in Bahrain and I could stay there even longer now that I didn't have to pay for a room at the hotel – even though it was cheaper there for me than for others.

I ended up staying seven months in Bahrain. Baby mentioned she knew of a lady who could get you a visa at a very good price, so I decided to buy a visa to be able to stay without any restrictions. I soon realised it was the same woman I had met before – Mary. I went to see her with Baby, who later left me alone with Mary to talk about the visa. I remembered my mum's advice to be careful about what I drank from strangers.

Mary was very friendly and talkative. After a while, she asked me if I wanted a drink and produced an opened can of coke from the kitchen. I took a sip and had an immediate reaction to it. I knew it was spiked. My senses were super heightened in those days! I went to the sink and poured the coke out while Mary went into the other room. When she came back, I had an empty can of coke sitting in front of me on the table. I felt in danger, so made an excuse to leave. Mary kept insisting I stay and have another drink but I walked to the door. Although my head was swirling a bit, I knew once I was out, I was safe.

I later spoke to someone about the incident. They knew of her and told me that they had heard that Mary spiked women's drinks when they visited her and then men came and had their way with the women while Mary collected money from the men. Because the women were drugged, they didn't realise what had happened to them and would go off home all relaxed without a clue. This is what was told to me. After leaving her home in a drowsy state, I thought it could be true.

I used to go to a local bookshop and hang out with the owner, reading books and chatting to him. The next day, I dropped in to tell him what had happened at Mary's house. He didn't say much, but it turned out he knew Mary well and they were friends! Baby had heard this from others and she told me that he would go and tell her what I said. I vowed not to see her after that, until one day, many months later, I bumped into her and she told me about a super party she was going to that included high officials. She was going with a few women and said I could come along and get a fee for just attending and would make extra if I danced. I needed the money so I accepted. I knew I had to be careful with Mary though. I knew what she was capable of.

The evening she was due to pick me up, I prepared myself. She was with a few other Bahraini women, who were all totally covered up in black abaya dress. I got out my black Versace bag, which I'd bought on sale at a super low price, and made sure I didn't have anything in it except my keys and comb – no passport or identification.

The ladies arrived at my flat and I was relieved they were happy, smiling women. I wasn't sure what Mary had told them about me, but it seemed an amicable meet-up. We left in a big four-wheel-drive driven by one of the ladies. Mary sat at the front and I sat in the back. It wasn't too far away, so when we got there, I cautiously got out with the others and followed them to an ordinary looking apartment block and was soon greeted by an Indian worker who was waiting to take us up in the lift to the party.

We entered quite a large space, although it didn't measure up to my expectations – after all, I had been in palaces. The furniture was moved away from the centre to create a space in the middle, and the furniture was all piled up on the outskirts of the room. The middle of the room was made up for the people to drink in a circle, with rugs and cushions scattered around. An authentic Middle-Eastern band was set up to play live on the other side of the room, which excited me. I decided to hang out with them once I received my fee for attending.

The band started up and all these Saudi men appeared, looking like they had just woken up with hangovers. There was lots of alcohol, food was brought out, and women were swooning over the men. I started drinking to relax but felt uneasy with the type of men there. Mary had said there would be Sheikhs – they looked like Bedouins from the desert, and drunk ones at that. I got up and had a dance and I was paid the fee that was promised – scattered over me in payment for my appearance.

There was a boy-girl dancing, of Philippine nationality, and he was getting the most attention from anyone there – the men were throwing money at him from all angles, and he loved it! I couldn't believe they preferred him to a woman! He was the life of the party and making a ton of money. I was shocked that an ordinary male dancing, acting so feminine, would be outdoing me. I had to admit I didn't feel like dancing for those inebriated men, so I did the one dance without effort, then stopped and sat at a distance from the group.

On the Persian rugs I noticed bottles of Johnny Walker whiskey had been placed on the floor for us, along with an assortment of nuts. I decided to have a few drinks to relax and stay closer to the band. They were more to my liking and one of the band members spoke English and was very attentive towards me. The night went on, and I conversed with him during his break. When his break was due to end, I turned around to see the room was empty. The women had disappeared suddenly. I had been so focused on talking with the band members, and one in particular, I was oblivious to the fact everyone had left the room. "Where did they all go?" I asked in surprise.

The drummer, whom I had taken a liking to, asked me if I knew what was going on. I didn't, so he explained that Mary was a pimp – the girls were brought for the men and she would get a fee. I was horrified and decided that I would never go near her again. So it was true about her!

I went to get my bag from where I had left it, but it wasn't there. I was a bit upset and asked people if they had seen it. Then one of the men – not one of the Saudi men but a Bahraini who turned up later to the party in western attire – told me that he saw Mary take my bag! On hearing this, my response was to scream out like a banshee. I screamed out her name, calling for her to bring back my bag. About five minutes later, my bag was back in the room like magic. I think Mary must have been hiding from me after she returned my bag. My money was still in there. I was so glad I didn't have any ID with me that night. I was sure that Mary was trying to find some information about me to make some trouble!

I decided that I would stick close to the drummer and asked him to give me a lift home afterwards. I wasn't going anywhere with Mary after this incident. An hour later, the women appeared again from the rooms and were ready to go home. Mary cautiously approached me and asked if I wanted a lift home, to which I boldly said, "No!" in a firm voice. She took off without a word and I left soon after with the band members. I was grateful that they helped me out.

When I arrived back home in Australia, I had an experience again with Mary – in a lucid dream. It was as real as being there! I was dreaming I was in a taxi, when suddenly I was awakened by a pain in my chest area. It was similar to my first experience – an entity taking the life out of me. It was as though my life was been strangled – a shadow was moving up and up, squeezing my life away. I was frozen. No movement was possible. It felt as though something was sitting on me – a heavy feeling of suffocating.

Luckily for me, I remembered how I'd dealt with it previously. I just needed to say a protection Buddhist mantra. I first visualised it in my mind, repeating it and moving it to my heart centre, then to my lips where I was able to shout out the mantra with such a force that I even scared myself!

When I regained control, I closed my eyes and was suddenly back in a taxi with Mary. I knew she was the culprit, as she had reached out to touch my arm. Pain radiated towards my heart. I boldly looked at her and spat at her face. I saw the saliva start to dissolve into her face like acid, burning. I shouted out to her, "Leave me alone and if you ever come near me again, you will regret it!"

When I next went back to Bahrain, I heard that she had gone to live in America. I was so happy that she was out of the island now and couldn't hurt me or anyone there again.

23

Relationship

I was working at an event one night when I met an older distinguished-looking man called Harold. It was during the spring season at the Flemington races and I was placed in an area solely for patrons that had purchased seating for those particular days. My job was to check their tickets and assist with their seating. A happy and smiling man approach me with his ticket and I took him to his reserved seating. I thought he was a lovely man, and continued on with my work.

As the day progressed, he came over frequently to where I was standing to have a quick chat between races. By the end of the day, I had told him about my previous trip to Dubai and a bit about myself and decided to give him my card with my telephone number, as we had gotten on so well that day.

He never called me that year, so I forgot him. However, the following year, when I went back to work at the same venue, he was waiting for me, eager to tell me about his latest trip to Dubai. He also told me he lost my card and wanted to contact me but couldn't. That was nice to know. Anyway, we hit it off again and were soon chatting about life events.

Harold and I had so much to talk about. He later asked me if he could meet me for lunch, as he was going to be in my area the following week, and I agreed. I remember walking up to the café we had organised to meet at, and I could see him pacing up and down in a nervous manner.

After this encounter, we started seeing each other for lunches, then after a couple of months we became more than friends. We went to each other's places on a regular basis.

It was lovely to be with someone who I felt a deep connection with. I felt he was my soulmate. However, our relationship was nothing short of a roller coaster ride – up and down, break-ups all the time and then make-up sex. I know we came together for a reason – for me to learn big lessons through my time with him – and I'm sure our experiences together would have shown him parts of himself he needed to see – perhaps his dark side. As Jungian psychology teaches, we all have to face and embrace.

There were times his personality changed so much that I envisioned venom coming out of his mouth – I was so affected by his words. At other times he was considerate and kind. He always said I was very deep when I talked about being a Soul in a physical body and discussed Buddhist philosophies with him. He mentioned he had never encountered anyone like me before and that I was the only woman who was able to touch him to the core through our lovemaking. He told me that he had never experienced such passion in his life.

I do believe that I gave away a lot of my power to him because I was so attached to him. And after a period had elapsed, I started to feel very disempowered in our relationship. I was so focused on him and the relationship working, that I could see he was becoming more powerful from it. He was starting to attract women to him and his confidence was quite apparent. I was putting him on a pedestal and he enjoyed all the attention from me, while his focus was soon on other women as well.

I put our differences down to the fact that he was working more from the head and I was working more from the heart. Our personalities were very different, but our connection to the Soul is what brought us together. I could see a part of him that I adored, when he was not in his head. The best times to see him on this level was when he was attending his favourite recreational sports and relaxed, away from work. He was so open-hearted at those times, it was like he had two different personalities. I was in love with his Spirit, yet his ego took over a lot of the time.

His position kept him ego-based, too. He had very good insight about people of all types and had to use his intellect and judgement to be good at his job – I suppose I was able to give him some food for thought about the Soul. I knew he would be promoted eventually, because he was extremely dedicated to his job and so honest in his position.

He was, I believe, one of my greatest teachers – he helped me see that I had self-worth issues that needed work. My buttons were pressed so much during our time together, which made me go search even more to discover myself! I used to see him as a wizard at times – there was a lot of power within him. I think he was aware of that, too.

I was studying Holistic Counselling when I met Harold. Once I completed that course, I went on to studying nursing. I thought it would be a good way to have a secure income. How wrong was I about that!

I took a few jobs as a personal carer during that time and they were all disastrous. When I did the night shifts, I was always left on my own. At the first place I worked, I had three aged-care residents buzz me at the same time and I had to prioritise which was more important: the one who was having trouble breathing, the one who fell on the bathroom floor, or the one that was saturated from bed-wetting and walking around with her underwear ready to fall off. There was also one that always tried to climb out of her bed and I spent hours calming her down. I was exhausted tending to her on the nights I worked.

It was too much for me, so one night so I raced upstairs to the living quarters to get a more superior worker to come and help me. What I got was an annoyed woman who I had woken up. I attended to the woman who couldn't breathe properly, using the reflexology method to relax her and get her to breathe. When I went to get my pay later, I found out she was fine. I was told I wasn't needed after that, because I couldn't cope on my own. Well, looking after everyone on your own at night wasn't easy.

The next place I worked was a retirement lodge. I worked mainly at night there – usually the shifts no one wanted. One time I was taking medications for my liver and I wasn't in the best of health – my immune system was low because of it. I had worked a few night shifts in a row and I really didn't want to do any more. The owner rang and convinced me to do another shift, this time saying I could bring my dog with me too. I had told him I couldn't leave my little dog alone again, so he agreed that I could leave him in the bedroom I used during my stay there overnight.

During the odd times I did work during the day, I had to know the residents' names and give them their tablets from the Webster packs, ready for them to take when they were seated for lunch. I really hated giving out tablets and made sure I always repeated their name before giving them out. You make one mistake, and that's it! One resident always made a joke with me when I repeated his name before giving him his medication – he stood out because he was livelier than the others.

When the owner asked me to work a final night shift before having my four days off, I went in as usual in the late afternoon and noticed that one of the employees was giving out liquors to the residents as a pre-dinner drink, so I went to help him out. The woman who was just finishing her shift came over to me and started hurling abuse at me for not going to do other more important chores, which I wasn't informed I had to do. I don't know what got into her, but it soon escalated in the kitchen. The chef started siding with her when he heard her argument. I didn't know how it started, but I was so mad at them and decided I wouldn't eat the dinner he cooked that night. The chef left after serving the food and I refused to touch his food due to how he spoke to me.

After the residents settled down for the night, I went looking for food for my dog and instead of picking up meat for him, I found cubed potatoes. That wouldn't do, so I decided I would give him slices of ham for dinner instead of the chicken tikka the chef made.

I usually only went to see the residents when they buzzed me, but that evening my intuition led me to check on one particular man. I opened his door and I was shocked to see him covered with vomit, the bathroom filled with vomit, and even the walls splattered with it! He was totally soiled as well.

I cleaned up the bathroom after double-gloving myself and took his PJs to put through the washing machine twice. It was such an awful chore. Once I finished, I went back to the man and gave him water to drink and asked if he was okay before going upstairs to find someone to help me. I had to be sure he was getting the best attention and I wasn't fully qualified to be doing anything more than keeping him hydrated and clean. There wasn't anyone available to help me. The husband of the manager opened the door and informed me the manager was out.

In desperation, I rang the owner and he told me he couldn't get there – it was the middle of the night, so I had to keep checking on the man during the night to make sure he was coping and comfortable. When I went back the second time, the man had again vomited all over himself, so I gave up on cleaning the floor. I changed the dressing gown he had on and gave him more water. The night dragged on – I checked on him hourly, worrying the whole time.

In the morning, when the staff turned up, the lady who had previously told me off came on for her shift and when I told her and the others what happened, they laughed about it, maybe because of how serious I looked while telling the story. The woman was chuckling away and I departed, disgusted at how I had been left to handle such a delicate situation. I decided that when I went in to get my wage for the four days work, I was going to leave.

Four days later, I went back to get my pay. It smelled like the carpets had been cleaned. The worker that I had helped give out the drinks told me that the morning I left, the whole place had broken out with gastro and everyone had been sick. There had been so much cleaning afterwards that everyone was run off their feet. *Now who has the last laugh?* I mused, thinking of the woman who laughed at me after the incident. He also told me that the man who I gave meds to and who was always joking with me had passed away from the gastro. This worker believed it was the food that made everyone sick. He said that he was sick with diarrhoea and vomiting for a few days too. He'd only just got back that morning.

I left with my paycheck in hand, vowing never to go back. On my way home, I thanked the universe for starting that argument that day, so I hadn't eaten the food. After all, I wasn't very well at that time and eating the food could have been disastrous for me and my dog, too! I do believe I was looked after that day.

24

Holiday with Symptoms

It was very hard to break ties with Harold, as we were very connected in spirit and we had been seeing each other for quite a few years. With so many buttons being pressed, however, I felt it was becoming unhealthy for me and intuitively knew I had to do something soon.

With my stomach churning and chest tightening too often, it soon became apparent something wasn't right. The truth came out eventually – he was with another woman. My gut had been right all along! I believe I stayed in the relationship for way too long – I was too dependent on him. When the truth reared its head, it shook me to the core. I knew it was time for me leave the relationship, after much torment to my Soul.

I decided to go back overseas to the Gulf. I always had a very strong sense of belonging there. The first destination I thought of was Bahrain. I was a terrible mess. I felt lost, betrayed and very unwell.

I started having lucid dreams at night – bats flying out of my chest area – and so many other strange symptoms. I felt I needed to get away, otherwise I believed I would died at home, due to a broken heart. My dog had passed away five months previously (he was very old and unwell at the end of his life but always my companion – I adored him). Now I was breaking ties with a man I had become attached to as well – it was all gone.

I told Harold I was going away and he was kind enough to help with a little money. I felt it was a much-needed trip. It had been quite a long time since I had last travelled. I didn't dare travel overseas whilst I was seeing Harold, as he was very jealous at times, so going to the Middle East was out of the question for a long time. But it was finally over.

My relationship, caring for my teenage son, and looking after my dog kept me home during that time. I also had studied nursing and dropped out just before I finished, due to the emotional upsets in my relationship. Also, it really wasn't suited to me because I tend to avoid medications, as I'm more into alternative and natural healing. The Holistic Counselling diploma I completed was really for my own therapy. I haven't gone out and used it as a career as yet, although I feel the like therapist at times with friends and family.

I decided Dubai would be my main destination instead of Bahrain as there was trouble there – riots and chaos. The ruling family was being challenged by Shiites who wanted to change the Sunni rulership. So, Bahrain was now too dangerous to visit for more than a short trip and Dubai was the next best place. I included Paris as well, as I had always wanted to go there and it didn't cost more for the ticket. I searched the internet for accommodation, checking every day over a whole month for a furnished room, before deciding on a Homestay and my first couch surfing experience in Dubai.

The day I boarded the plane I had a bad cough, which worsened during the flight. That was the start of my health problems. Once I landed in Dubai, my lungs were filled with mucus. I remember checking into a hotel room with a cold air conditioner and I couldn't work out how to adjust the temperature. My cough got even worse after that.

I contacted the host where I was to stay in Dubai – my host was a hip Indian yoga instructor. He directed me to his apartment, and when I arrived he pointed to a foam mattress next to his bed that I was to use for the following five days. I had found him on the Couchsurfing site, but it was a mistake to stay with him while I was in a vulnerable and sickly state. I could say I was taken advantage of whilst I was extremely ill – I didn't have any energy to do anything about it.

On the fifth day a lovely guy I had also contacted on the internet about accommodation turned up and showed me a vacant flat he had for an investment. It wasn't being used, so he offered it to me for no money. He wasn't even staying there. He told me that he wanted to help me out as he felt that I was a nice person – we had spent a couple hours chatting in a hotel lobby, sipping tea and eating Arabic treats.

My cough eased for a while after my couch-surfer host suggested a cough elixir called Propolis, which he took at times for his asthma. I noticed my cough became more manageable when I took it for a couple of weeks. It really did help – actually, it was a lifesaver!

My new friend, Ben, not only offered me the use of his investment flat, but also took me out to clubs and restaurants. He loved dancing too, so I was extremely pleased that I could dance as well as I had indicated to him. He always told me later that whenever he thought of me, it was of when we were out dancing – he always enjoyed our nights on the dance floor.

I had been in Dubai almost four weeks and was due to leave for Paris, so I arranged to meet Ben at the airport. He was arriving after one of his regular travels away. He told me he would be there early in the morning if I wanted to see him before I took off for Paris.

On the morning of my flight, he bought me breakfast and also gave me some American money to help me out in Paris. I told him I was going to sell my gold bangle and it was worth four hundred dollars. I asked him if he wanted to buy it from me. He thought about it for a few minutes, then did a wonderful thing – he decided to give me that amount and not take my gold bangle. He knew my situation and just wanted to help. Also, I presume that amount wasn't a great deal to him as he was quite wealthy. It was a lovely gesture on his part, once again.

On my flight to Paris, the middle-aged lady seated next to me understood that it was my first visit to France – it showed in my anxious tone. I wasn't sure where to go to take the train to the host's apartment in Belleville. So, once we proceeded to disembark, she said that she would accompany me onto the train. I followed her, quite relieved to purchase a train ticket to my destination, which she paid for herself, refusing my money for it. She beckoned me to follow her onto another platform for the train. After some time, she instructed me where to get off, as she had arrived at her stop. I thanked her for her help and generosity and kept my ears open to the announcement of which platform was coming up. I had arrived finally and walked into the bustling street, noticing the area had a strong Arabic presence. I felt at home!

I soon discovered that the people living in that area were predominantly Arabic, with a few Chinese shop owners too. The first few days alone there, I was either confronted by an Algerian or Tunisian man wanting to befriend me. I could see that they were men on the prowl – mainly illegal immigrants in survival mode. It was actually quite annoying, as they pestered me to go and have coffee with them. The first guy was okay until after the coffee and long walk. He then started to pester me to allow him to give me his number to call him. He finally left me alone when I agreed to call him the next day, which I only said so I could get rid of him.

The next guy was harder to get rid of – he thought because he was a lot younger than I was, I would pay for his drink. He nagged me until he convinced me to have a coffee with him. We went into a café and he immediately ordered a shot of whiskey and a coffee and I then ordered myself a coffee. When I went to pay for it, the café worker expected me to pay for his as well. I said no and only paid for mine. The guy then had to pay for his own drinks. I think he knew the manager who was suggesting I pay for the guy, until I flatly refused.

I walked off, hoping he would get the message that I wasn't interested; however, he wouldn't leave me alone. He insisted that I stay with him. I had to walk a bit faster after an hour of his trying to convince me we should get together. It was starting to get annoying, as he wouldn't accept that I wasn't interested even when I told him bluntly. I was feeling a bit anxious and had to get rid of him. I saw a cinema complex ahead and ran into it and hid. He didn't see where I ran to, as he was lagging behind by then. He sped up when he noticed I disappeared suddenly, but by then, I had escaped. I watched him walk past visibly annoyed – I was very relieved to be rid of the pest! Every day I was in that area alone, I would have some guy tailing me.

The apartment I stayed at was owned by an older French woman who worked from home. She spoke fluent English. On the day I arrived, when she first greeted me at her place, she had a male friend with her. I suppose he was there as a precaution and he left soon after, once he saw I was safe to stay in her home. I had a lovely room, facing the main street and the bed was so comfy!

It was a lovely place. She did have cats though, and I had to contend with cat litter in the tiny toilet space – the smell of urine was off-putting. The kitchen was out of bounds by lunchtime, so if I wanted to prepare food, I would run out and buy some salad mixture and get back to make my lunch for the day, otherwise I bought quiches or croissants.

I was doing some push-ups in my room after two days there, when I noticed something irritating my bra under the wire part. I got up and felt around the area and found a lump. It was quite large and I thought maybe if I squeezed it might get rid of what was in it. Nope – it looked a bit green, and I knew deep down it was something more but I wanted to ignore it. I decided I wasn't going to focus on it and get on with my holiday.

Paris turned out to be great; I met some interesting locals. One afternoon whilst out shopping, I met a man at the department store Lafayette. I had just purchased two pairs of adorable shoes on my Visa card and I was happily carrying my shopping bag along the ground floor towards the exit, smiling to myself about my purchase, when I noticed a middle-aged man smiling back at me. He was seated at the champagne and juice bar and I caught his body language telling me to join him at the bar. I thought *Why not?* So I put my parcel down on a seat next to me and engaged in conversation with this well-dressed man in his sixties, who introduced himself as Francois. He spoke fluent English and was very articulate.

I was quite impressed with Francois and it wasn't long before he invited me out to dine with him. We met on several occasions. He took me to exquisite restaurants and bars. He was a real gentleman. Although the chemistry wasn't there, I did enjoy his company. Alas, once I left, even though he gave me his details and said he would contact me, he didn't respond after I told him by email the news of my diagnosis. I guess he just wanted happy news and I never mentioned the lump to him when we were together.

I also met a charming younger man at the local café near my accommodation in Paris and he hardly spoke any English. He was Algerian, had crossed the border illegally, and was peddling cigarettes to earn some money in an area of Paris that was quite run-down and filled with immigrants. He noticed me sitting at the table and smiled at me. Because I smiled back at him, he decided to come up to my table and sit next to me and began speaking in fluent French.

I replied to him broken French telling him I don't speak French, I speak English. I knew a little French as I had studied it for a year and I knew Arabic from my travels to the Gulf so I was able to converse with him in a mixture of English, Arabic and French – somehow he understood me! He was different to the others, not so needy and I felt he had a beautiful soul. I felt comfortable with him. I felt at ease and relaxed in his presence and from that encounter, we were able to strike up a friendship. I explained to him how I wanted to see Paris, but didn't know how to get around so he offered to guide me around the city.

From then on, every day he came to meet me and showed me the sights of Paris. We took the metro and went on long walks. I was so relieved as I had been afraid to travel by train thinking I would get lost. I'm aware I get a bit of anxiety and panic when I'm in a strange place and don't know my way around.

Every day we visited all the famous places, the Eiffel Tower, Montmartre, the Arc de Triomphe and some lovely gardens. I felt very safe around him and trusted him too. We went for lunches and shared the cost of the meal as he was just surviving and I was on a tight budget travelling as well. He would then head off to his job selling cigarettes in an area called Pigalle. I went there one day and it was so unattractive to me, filled with illegal immigrants selling everything and anything. I didn't stay there long. The energy wasn't as nice as the main tourist spots.

I only saw him during the day so I really didn't know whether he was married or in a relationship, but as I was only interested in him being a friend that didn't matter to me. His name was Laide'. He had such a lovely energy and I felt very light around him and happy he came into my life when I needed a friend.

I moved into another area near the Moulin Rouge after five days and I got the lady of the house to call him, to tell him that I had moved to her place for next six days. This family included a couple in their late twenties and their three young children under the age of eight. I was staying in the son's room whilst he stayed at a friend's. They were very hospitable towards me and I felt very comfortable staying with them and really enjoyed their girls' company. I dined with them every night, as it was included with my accommodation.

Laide' would come over every morning and meet me at the nearby café and we would go and explore the area or sit in the beautiful gardens close-by basking in the sun. He was so easy to be with, even with not many words exchanged.

One night whilst eating with the family a Moroccan man dropped in to visit them that was married to one of her close friends. They told him I loved to dance and asked if he knew of any place he could take me to dance. He didn't speak English too well but I trusted him because he was a friend of my hosts. I decided to go with him to a club nearby. He explained, as we were walking there, that it had Middle Eastern music and his friend worked there.

At the entrance he spoke with the doorman and a woman asked me for an entrance fee of sixty Euros. I was very surprised and asked why? She said, that they include a small bottle of whisky on the table. I didn't want to drink whisky and I didn't have that type of money on me anyway. I tried to convince them to let me in at a cheaper rate without the drinks. I'm a good dancer I told them, thinking they may let me in. I had to give it a go, however that didn't work. I thought to myself I will have to give dancing in Paris a miss this time.

I looked at the man that brought me there and said, "no" and started walking back to my place with him following slowly behind me, trying to convince me it was worth going to. I had a feeling this guy was going to get free entrance or some pay-off for taking me there. I felt somehow I couldn't attract what I wanted, it was more of a tease to be taken to a club and not to able to enter. I guess if energies are not flowing and there is something the body is fighting then, it would be harder to attract much outside of you.

I chose to ignore the lump on my breast and enjoy the rest of my holiday there. I went to many open market stalls close by that were amazing – brimming with fresh cheeses, vegetables and fruit. The market at Belleville was the best one I had ever come across with so much fresh food, opening times were early morning till after lunch. There were a few small household appliances and clothing on offer on certain days.

Once it was time to leave and I told Laide' I had to go back to Dubai he was very sad to see me go and pleaded for me to stay longer. I told him I couldn't stay, I had very limited funds. I tried explaining that I had found a lump in my breast. I'm not sure if he understood, but I told him I wasn't well and had to go home. I had my flight booked back via Dubai, then back home to Melbourne. I had to deal with my lump eventually, but I was determined to finish off my trip first.

On arrival in Dubai, I tried calling Ben but there was no answer so I decided to spend the whole night on the couches in the lounge area of the airport. I had landed at 2AM and by the time I got through customs it was too late to think of a room. I thought I could save some money this way anyway. In the morning I got through to Ben and he asked me to check into a hotel and he would see me the following day. But the following day he didn't answer his phone and I started to panic as the hotel was quite expensive and that meant I had to pay for another day if he didn't come and get me. I had to think of something.

I remembered there was a gentleman that had offered me a room previously and his place was near to where I was staying, in an area called Discovery Gardens. I decided I would call him and go over there and wait until I heard from Ben again. I caught the public transport over and he picked me up from the train terminal and I went to his flat to wait for Ben. He didn't know that I wasn't planning to stay at his place. I just said, I wanted to look at the room. It was an awkward time waiting for hours with a strange Indian man hovering around me. I prayed that Ben would call soon as it was starting to become dark and goodness knows what the sleeping arrangements were going to be!

Ben finally did call me early evening and told me he would be there soon. Once I finished with the phone call, I told the man I had to go and left quickly with him confused as to where I was going. All I told him was that my friend had arrived as I went out the door. I then walked to the nearby flat owned by Ben and waited outside the door for about close to an hour.

Ben arrived all flustered in a cab, he explained that he had been in an incident with his car earlier that day and it was a miracle no-one was hurt. I thought that maybe, when he was praying after the incident, he thought of me and said to himself, if I get out of this I'll go and get her – maybe that's why he rang me back. I have heard stories about Expatriates living in the Middle Eastern countries that get into traffic accidents where another local is involved and is hurt, then they get arrested and thrown into jail and stay there until their court hearing and then big amounts of money may be demanded as well.

I could see on his face that he had been scared by the incident that occurred and needed to do the right thing and help me out now. After all he, did say he would. Anyway, it all turned out good. Ben left in the cab soon after and happy he could help me out again, and I was feeling relieved that I had his place to sleep at once again. I didn't tell him where I had been waiting before he arrived.

The next night I went back to the night club I had recently discovered nearby that played Middle Eastern music for a dance. I had a few weeks to go before I left Dubai, and I wanted to go to visit Lucy, my girlfriend who was living in Bahrain. I had met her years before in Melbourne and had taken her to Bahrain. She was now living and working in there. She invited me there after she stayed with me in Dubai my first week back from Paris.

We did have a good time, dining and dancing and chatting about what was going on in our lives since the last time we had seen each other in Australia. Her son had been in the same class as my son and they were friends, so I first met her through them. I always wanted to live in Bahrain myself and after I took Lucy there, I realised she was going to follow through with my dream instead.

I still had with me the thick gold chain that my friend the Sheikh gave me when he was in Australia for the Olympic Games in 2000. I was getting short of money by now, so even though I was going to stay at my friend Lucy's place. I thought it may be time to sell it as well as the price of gold was very high there and I would be able to enjoy my last leg of the holiday with ease.

There was unrest in all of the Middle East then, so it wasn't appropriate to go to Bahrain for long. I only went to see my friend Lucy and because it was my favourite Gulf destination for so many reasons. Also I wanted to meet her Egyptian boyfriend who she spoke of many times. They were both working in the education system.

While I was there, though, it became very uncomfortable. Lucy went to work and I went out exploring the island during the day. She would question me on my whereabouts every time after she got home. She was worried that I would be kidnapped there because I was out and about. I wasn't afraid to be out, just had to be cautious as usual and go with my gut. In the end, I had to leave her place as her partner tried to be too friendly one night. After an incident unfolded, and he denied it to Lucy once, I told her about it. I tried not to tell her but she had suspicions and I couldn't hold back after she questioned me about why I locked the bedroom door.

Tensions rose in the flat and with only two days left in Bahrain I decided I would leave and enjoy the remainder I had there going to the clubs. The nightlife in Bahrain was the best part for me. I could have some fun and dance without interference. Lucy was so paranoid, she even locked me in the flat one of the days until she came home.

The parting was tense. Lucy suggested I just take the first plane out, but I wasn't going to leave without exploring more and having a dance. It turned out I had the best time dancing the same night I had left her place. The fact that I now had to pay for accommodation pushed me to sell my gold chain. I went into town that afternoon and saw many dealers, to hear what they were offering and get the best price. This way I had an idea of its value. By the afternoon, I settled with a Bahraini family-run business who didn't hassle me as much as the other shop owners. I sold it for a nice sum. I guess the figure they offered was what was in my head and I had enough of checking out prices by then.

It felt great to have rolls of notes in my bag for a change. I decided to go and spoil myself so I went and had my hair and nails done at a beauty salon that I had been to many times on previous visits years earlier. I knew the owner so she allowed me to leave my luggage there for the day. The women working there were from India and Malaysia and on very low wages. I always tried to help them out with a little money whenever I came across them.

There was one lady that never smiled the whole time I was being pampered and I spoke to her later and asked about her life and she told me that she hadn't been paid for a couple of months. She lived at the salon with the others but was struggling with sending her family money to live in Malaysia.

I stayed at the salon with the ladies all afternoon and listened to all their stories about their struggles with surviving on a small wage. As I had sold my gold chain, I was able to tip them for their services a bit more than they expected from me. The Malaysian woman was starting to open up more in conversation as the hours together progressed. I was in the kitchen when this lady went to get something to eat and I saw it was only plain rice. I saw how her teeth looked very separated and needed work. I could see that she was lacking in nutrition.

I asked her if I could borrow her mobile to call someone I knew and she said she didn't have much credit on her phone. So I decided to go to the grocery store and buy a few things for her after that. I bought a few treats and a phone recharge for her. I also gave her a few dinars as well. Once she received this, she was smiling and I was so pleased I could do something for her. I always do this whenever I met women working in poor conditions and they tell me their story. If I can lift their spirits up for a little while then I will do it, even though my finances have been on survival mode, it's never as bad as these women I have met, that only receive a paltry sum for the work they do.

Later that evening I rang my taxi friend, who I had met on one of my travels in the city complex. He came and picked me up and took me to a lovely hotel complex. I had a wad of money in my pocket and I could enjoy my time and buy myself a glass of wine and whatever I wanted.

At the hotel I noticed there was a reggae band playing and lots of people enjoying the atmosphere, I immediately relaxed, went and bought myself a drink. After having a dance towards the front of the band area, I noticed a younger man had his eye on me and approached me for a dance. We soon chatted for a bit and this man, named Mohammed, asked me if I wanted to go to another place and dance to Salsa music. I agreed as he had a car and taxis can be quite expensive and I did want to try out a few places.

We soon arrived at a hotel complex, where there was a small bar with a dance floor. It wasn't too busy, and we bought our own drinks and went onto the dance floor. I couldn't really get into the groove of the music. Mohammed had been taking lessons so he was enjoying it, while I was feeling it wasn't my style of dance. I was on my way to the ladies shortly after, when I saw groups of men going into the lift and I asked where they were going. I was informed there was an Arabic club upstairs, so I decided I would go up to see the place. I was totally taken by it. The music playing was Gulf style and it was pumping! That was more to my liking! I just had to collect my new friend and bring him up here I thought. I asked the doorman if it was okay and he nodded Yes!

I went back down to my new friend and told him to come up with me, he wasn't too happy, but obliged. We were seated next to a few Saudi men wearing their traditional thobe. I told my friend, I was going to dance and left him there. I jumped onto the stage filled with only men dancing, most of them already intoxicated. I soon was in a spell with the music soaring through me and I danced well – so well that the microphone was switched on and the man behind it was asking who I was? He was very impressed by my dancing and others were all clapping.

My new friend Mohammed talked with people nearby and they were sending him drinks and offering him whatever treats they had in front of them, mainly fruits. He was so happy to have all this attention from men that he had thought weren't very nice. It was because he was a Yemeni working in Saudi and his pay was very low, even though he had a professional job and was born in Bahrain. He had no health cover either because he wasn't a Saudi, so he did have a lot to say about the discrimination, how Saudi's had the best jobs and conditions and no-one else had rights there. He told me how a family member couldn't get treatment for his cancer because he didn't have any medical cover. I guess he wanted to blame the Saudi people as a whole. I think this night was an eye-opener for him though. He was having a fantastic time with them now and could see it wasn't about the people. It was the system only, the government. These men were very friendly and generous in nature.

We stayed till the end of the night and when we were leaving everyone was praising him for having such a lovely girlfriend. They thought we were together and I think that was a smart move by him to agree too. As I was leaving the dance floor, an older gentleman came to me to give me his worry beads. They were made of lovely beads with silver bits in them. He wanted me to have a memento from him, to say thanks for dancing for them.

Mohammed and I went to an island resort for coffee and sat outside in the lounge seating until the early hours, just chatting. He was a lovely person to be around. Much younger than I, but so very wise. When it was almost light we went back to town. I went to the front of his hotel and took his number, promising we would do this again when I returned. I then went into a fast-food outlet near there and stayed there for an hour or so until it was a reasonable time to call my taxi cab driver – a new friend who was driving me around Bahrain on a cheaper rate. He drove me to a place that I had discovered was offering a very good price for a whole apartment. I booked in for my last night there, but first I had to go and collect my travel case from the salon.

That last night Mohammed had gone back to Saudi, so I decided to find a new place to dance at that was closer to where I was now staying. It was quite central to the nightlife. That evening I walked around and went into a bar that was giving out free drinks for the first couple of hours to ladies. It was something that most bars did for ladies on the island, usually on a designated night. This means women get drinks super cheap for a few hours. Some places give you a few free vouchers or free basic wine or champagne all night. It depends on the place. It's a good way of attracting more women into the place. Then the men will follow in droves and spend up big. In the Gulf, the local women mostly stay home so it's mainly female expats that are out at the clubs or bars.

After a few drinks, I walked to a nearby hotel. I could hear music, so I went in to see what was happening. I noticed chairs set back from the stage and I sat down to watch the ladies. There were women dancing in long gowns or short dresses on the stage, all trying to impress the men in the audience, especially the tables closer by. These tables were usually allocated to the big spenders, as they would give the women flowers that are made into garlands to show them that they had their attention. The women would dance enticingly to receive more flowers from them. Each garland cost ten dinar to buy for the dancer, and they would get five for each one they returned to management at the end of the night. If you impressed a guy, he might keep buying them all night for you.

I asked if it was okay for me to dance and the women were happy to allow me, as I was a foreigner and not a threat. But once I got up to dance, I soon had everybody's attention, which they didn't expect to happen. The ladies were laughing, they couldn't believe a foreigner could dance better than them. Men sent me garlands of red flowers. I said to the woman who tried to drape them over me, "will I be getting the money for them?" She said, "No," so I refused to take them from the men then. The woman went and told the manager and he came and took me off the stage. The men in the audience were looking a bit puzzled to why I wouldn't take their token of appreciation. The manager asked me to sit down on a chair that was further away from the tables of men. But by this time, I was ready to go home. I wasn't going to stay if I couldn't dance – especially if I couldn't get paid like the other women. So I walked back to my room happy that I wasn't going to be exploited by the club.

The next day I took the plane back to Dubai for my last two weeks there. Ben had left a key out for me, but I'd already had one cut – in case he made me wait for him again.

I still had some money from the sale of my gold chain, so as there were lots of sales then in Dubai I went shopping and bought some nice clothes hugely discounted. I also bought lots of healthy food, salads and juices every day.

I was having some symptoms again with my chest filling with fluid and I had some antibiotics brought to me by a guy I had dinner with a couple of times during my time in Dubai. I had mentioned my symptoms to him and he met me at a local restaurant for a meal one night and brought me the medications. He talked of taking me to a Reiki session but that never happened. He was busy with work. I also still had the magical syrup I first bought when I arrived in Dubai compliments to the couch surfer host who put me onto to the product.

I went back to my favourite club to dance nearby that had Arabic music playing once a week. It had full capacity that night. It was a popular place and very expensive if you were drinking. I went earlier in the evening and was expecting a Swedish friend to turn up later. I had met her there previously and we always got together for a dance, as she was alone as well, although she had numerous admirers. She was in her early twenties.

I always had a drink at home before I went out, just to chill, and as soon as the music started I was fine dancing alone on the dance floor. I always got an invite to join a table of people after that. This one night I met a young man who came over and wanted to dance with me. He just adored my dancing and asked me to join his group afterwards. It turned out he was paying for all the drinks that night and they didn't stop coming. I didn't know who he was but we got on so well, that we danced together the whole night. My Swedish girlfriend turned up and was quite impressed. She had an Arabic man with her as usual, but that didn't stop her from coming over and asking for my new friend's number! Naturally he gave it to her. She was a real go-getter!

I left after giving him my contact details and went home, my symptoms were getting worrisome now. My left arm had swelling underneath the armpit. I knew it was getting serious now. I had brought a rose crystal with me and intuitively placed it under my arm-pit that night, it helped me sleep. The next day I was a complete wreck. I had to pack but was so tired from the night out, I stayed in bed most of the day and decided to pack once I felt better.

I got a call from my new friend that evening, the one I had just met at the Arabic club. He was driving to another club that night with his pilot friend and asked me to come out with them. He had told his friend about me and wanted him to see me dancing. He passed the phone over to his friend and I explained to his friend that I couldn't as I was leaving in the morning for home and needed to pack. This was my last night. I was leaving in the morning to go home.

25

Home and Cancer Scare

In Melbourne I headed to my doctor within a couple of days to show her the lump on my left breast. She immediately wrote a referral and sent me to the hospital for testing. Of course, the finding was breast cancer. I always knew I had it but didn't want to rush home to ruin my first holiday away in a decade. I had thought to myself, if I was going to die, I may as well enjoy my time away first.

Well, from that moment I was going for biopsies, having lumpectomies, bone scanning, all sorts of testing. I was going crazy! I would have surgery, then soon after another lump would come up, again and then again. I felt that having all the anxiety through all this didn't help me either – the tests and all the hospital visits were turning into a nightmare for me. I was so confused as to how I couldn't just have had a lumpectomy and heal, but it soon became out of control. I never believed it could happen to me, but it did!

I remember days at home looking for remedies to help the inflammation reduce when I had flare ups in my chest area that were very painful. I used cabbage leaves that I put in olive oil and applied to my throbbing breasts!

My older sister had breast cancer before me, but I never thought I would get it, not even after I learnt that my father's sisters both had it and had one died a few years back. I still didn't think it would ever happen to me as I thought as I was doing lots of gym work and applying daily meditation into my lifestyle. I thought I was eating an adequate diet. But I realised, after many operations and internet searches and talking to professionals along with attending workshops on food for health, that I was lacking in nutrients due to my previous liver problems. I didn't absorb the vital vitamins as well, therefore needed more juicing and vegetables to be introduced. I was constantly on the internet doing searches on how I could heal from food and nutrients I needed.

I even went and had a few sessions of art therapy with students needing to complete their hours to obtain their final results! I remember the lady I went to where I drew images of a snake and there were eggs around it. I then proceeded to colour it and the eggs had black speckles through it and the therapist asked me what did I need, to change the outcome? Intuitively, I wanted to fill them in pink after.

I knew that love was needed to heal even then, but somehow I didn't know how to do this still – I had too much grief and anger held in me – I had to process it. I guess this was how my Soul wanted me to learn.

I was so distraught and prayed whenever I could to help me through the whole nightmare of it. I hated going to the waiting room and feeling the vibes of everyone waiting to see the doctor for their results. In the end I had to say to the receptionist, I'll be waiting outside the room, call me when you need me. I also suggested to the receptionist that they should play some soothing music as there was so much tension in the waiting room.

This went on for over three years, removing tumours from the left breast and then the other side started showing symptoms after as well. It was like popcorn, so many came up, like the pictures I drew with the eggs of the snake. So, in the end, my surgeon told me if I didn't have the mastectomy I wouldn't have any skin left on my breast to even have a breast. That's when I had to finally agree to having it even though I was so against doing this to my body. My breasts were beautiful to me and I had to chop them off – at least what was under them.

The day of the surgery I thought I would change my mind and I had two surgeons on either side of me waiting for me to change my mind back again. I prayed to God to help me. I needed a miracle, but nothing happened. The nurse came to me and spoke to me of how important it was for me and I weighed it all up and decided that there was no point in resisting it. I finally agreed to have the mastectomy.

On waking up after the operation I was in pain. It seemed like something was jabbing at me, not sure what it was, but this is what kept me in hospital longer than usual. I felt like a part of me was lost forever and I was grieving over it, it was so devastating.

I remember when I was sent to another area of the hospital after a few days in the main part of the hospital, it was for patients needing more time at hospital. I was in my room very upset at how my whole life unfolded when a nurse came in and saw the tears streaming down my face.

She sat down and told me a story that really moved me about her husband. He was a handsome man and she loved him so much but he wasn't as loving towards her as she would have liked him to be. He being very handsome had many female admirers and flirted with them constantly. One day at work acid had spilt on him and it was mainly on his face, he was severely burnt and spent many months in the burns unit at hospital. He thought his life was over as now his looks were gone, he felt useless and insignificant without his looks now.

The nurse, whom I'll call an angel told me that, because she loved him before, she still had the same love for her husband after, and knew that now he may learn to really understand love. She didn't care that his looks were gone, his heart was still the same, he was the man she fell in love with. She explained how now, her husband stays at home and cares for their child while she goes to work. He even makes her lunch and their love is so much stronger than before. This story was so touching, it helped me cope better with the loss of what I saw was a significant part of me. It enabled me to really go back to listening to my intuition even more after that story of her love.

I was always on the spiritual path since a child but because I didn't have much support around me with this area, and because I didn't feel I fitted in to society's expectations, I was lost trying to find the real authentic me. The only thing I loved was dancing. Nothing else moved me like that, besides Spirit, which was always shown to me through dance anyway.

I thought about my past relationship with the father of my children and how circumstances changed in our relationship and how it ended. I loved working with my ex-partner Mario, especially when we had the entertainment venue – that was a dream job around music and dance. Our relationship had ended because he was addicted to horse gambling and, in fact, he lost almost everything we owned because of it. There were also many times he spent away from home claiming to be busy – not so I later found out.

I had gone overseas back in 1997 when we separated and came back to nothing. He had sold off any property left with my name on it and was already living with a new woman. My son and I were homeless after that. My daughter had gone to Queensland for some rehab herself and to start her new life there. My brother allowed us to live with him in a tiny room built at the back of his house. I had so much anger come up when I realised what happened and I found it tough to survive. Mario wasn't even giving me child support – after a couple of payments he decided he wouldn't bother helping.

After that, I soon slipped into a deep depression and was only just surviving – I was frozen with deep despair and anxiety and couldn't even work. I felt lost, abandoned, and didn't know how I was going to work. My life was based on living as authentically as possible and now I couldn't even eat properly! Mario had moved on: he had a new partner and family.

From having many properties and businesses to living in poverty was such an extreme situation. I sure got a big kick up my backside from the universe! I still had to heal from all the traumas of my whole life – and now this. I looked at what happened as my Karma. It did take me a long time to learn how to forgive him. Letting go has taking the burden off me as well emotionally.

I believe the universe will give back what I lost three-fold, eventually. I've been working on changing my inner world to bring me a more satisfying outer world for many years. I look at what happened as the universe's way of taking me away from the material world, which distracted me from my soul lessons, from my inner world. After losing everything I started living simply and really began working through my inner demons and the inner rage of all my life experiences that I had repressed deep down and amounted to many years of depression and anxiety. I never took anti-depressants as I felt that my depression was about me losing control of my life and I needed to find my own way back. This is where meditation really helped. I remember for many years I hardly smiled because I lost all confidence in myself. The only thing that made me happy was dancing and because I was good at it, I would always be the first on the dance floor. This is one place where I wasn't afraid to be me!

I've had eight surgeries, a nipple reconstruction and fat transfer, I hope that is the final operation. I'm satisfied with how my new breasts look now. The Royal Womens' in Melbourne is a great hospital and the plastic surgery team too. I was always was happy with my plastic surgeon, Mr Dean Trotter. He is such a kind, caring man who listens to what you say, I love that, I felt that he is considerate of me as a person and I am respected.

I have to thank the nurses and surgeons at the Royal Melbourne Hospital too. They did the best they could for me – I understand that they may have found me difficult as a patient as I made choices that they didn't expect. I chose not to do Chemotherapy, or Radiotherapy, or take Tamoxifen tablets. I tried half a tablet for two weeks and was going out of my mind! My body didn't want this and I had to listen more to what my body was telling me now.

I did my research on what others were taking instead and weighing up what felt right and seeing a nutritionist. I know that everything that happened was for a reason and I had to know what that was. I was tired of abusing my body and Soul. I had to find out why I was going through this, otherwise I think I would not survive in this body.

This was what I needed to learn to get past it.

26

Dance Therapy Classes — The Answer!

While I was going through all the surgeries, I asked the universe to help me find what I needed to get through this – I'd just had enough! A close friend did a dance therapy course with me previously, and suggested I go to a dance therapy workshop that was coming up. I agreed to go to this workshop as I was now trying everything for the cancer to stop!

I went to the class run by a well-known movement teacher from the States who was visiting Melbourne every year to run workshops in Carlton. It was quite an active workshop and I focused on following with the theme of it – about weaving movement with our own meaning and seeing it unravel as the day went on.

The next day each student had to perform their story. That second day, watching the others on stage, I could see how unique everyone was in their own interpretation of how to perform their piece. It was interesting to watch how the unfolding of the first day flowed into the next as a finale.

When it was my turn to perform, I wasn't sure what I wanted to do, but I allowed my body to take over. I started on the floor moving in silence, then going with whatever arose within me. I used different levels to move, high and low movements, rolling on the floor, flowing, using strength in my arms and legs to proceed to running to the corners of the room. I wanted to use the whole space before me, it felt like a jigsaw puzzle at first. I was using my dance moves to get around the room, pirouetting here there and everywhere. I used the Laban method I had learnt through my Grad Dip training in movement and dance. Finally, after much expended energy, I collapsed to the floor and then let go, not knowing what was about to happen soon after.

I came to a sitting position on the floor and moving my arms up high and back down slowly and then my hands took over and made a shape of the heart, my fingers drew into a shape of a heart. The message of love came to me, this is what my answers was! I had to give and receive love – this is how I was going to heal.

Once I left that evening, I had confirmation of what I needed to do, open my heart again. I believe this started me on the road to recovery to heal myself, what helped me understand how heal my breast cancer – after all it is in the Heart Chakra and this does relate to love. I have read so many books on love and interpretations from many authors of what the meaning is – the answer I got was the one I needed for me to heal. I do believe that reading on a subject without experiencing it, makes it harder to understand the real depth of meaning. I've been reading self-help books all my life, attended many workshops and courses, and it's only when I had deep suffering come to me that I learnt the meaning from a Soul level. Maybe I chose to learn this way, but I wish I didn't have to lose a part of my anatomy for it.

I know this now. I will not judge too quickly as before. I understand everyone has their own story. I know my preference is to have more uplifting positive people around me now. I don't need dramas anyone. It's about being at ease so you don't attract disease.

When a relationship or friendship becomes toxic I have to let go of them without blaming anyone. I understand it's about learning about my comfort zone and being surrounded by lightness and peace instead of drama. Life will test you at times to see if you have learnt.

Whenever I let go of someone, then I am making room for another to enter. I will always listen to my own answers coming from within. I know, if I look, I will find them.

You have to be kind to yourself first!

27

Dakini Dance – My Performance

At the time I was going through all my surgeries I decided I would offer to dance for a charity event for abused children in India headed by an organisation here in Melbourne. I wanted to prove to myself that I still had passion left in my dance, I needed to see for myself how good I was and this way I could I get feedback from others if I was still a passionate dancer. I needed to prove to myself that I should still follow my bliss!

I was involved with a group for Holistic Counsellors through Facebook and one of the members was advertising for anyone interested in performing for a charity event to contact her. I thought it over and decided I would do a dance in honour of the Dakini Goddess in Tibetan Buddhism. I never forgot that my martial arts teacher – the one with whom I had the Enlightenment experience with – always thought of me as a living Goddess. This is called Dakini in Buddhism. Dakinis are energetic beings in female form. They are messengers of wisdom, of beauty and able to move freely in space and to impart the wisdom of realisation as female consorts to the male counterpart in union.

The charity performance was only a matter of weeks away and I had decided on music and the choreography for the dance. I chose a Lorenna McKenna instrumental tune, that sounded very sensual and reminiscent of snake charmers playing to the cobras and how they moved in synchronicity to the music. I wanted to flow and move as one. It was the only tune I could think of that could depict how I wanted to deliver my Dakini dance.

Earlier, on the day, I attended the Doncaster playhouse, a lovely old building hired for community performances, to get directions of my cue and to organise which lighting was to be used for each performance. It was filled with an audience of over a hundred paying patrons who were going to see various artists performing.

That night, there were many performers and it was a very professional line-up, all receiving great responses from the audience. I only rehearsed the song a few times as I already imagined how I want to dance it. I just needed to fit the music into my moves so I listened to it and worked out the routine. The beginning, the middle and the ending. I worked on the beats of the music to my hip swings and use of space and levels. I used my arms freely as I always do, without much choreography involved, it was coming from my inner core of my Soul.

Once I was satisfied that these moves depicted me as the living Goddess I would perform. I had to have an outfit too, so decided on whatever was in my wardrobe. I was just to wear a long black tight-fitting dress that had some stretch in it, and then just added a colourful scarf to my accentuate my hip movements. That was my costume! I always prepare at the last minute. I do procrastinate, but in the final moments with my good imagination skills, I can come up with a satisfactory result.

When the introduction was announced, I came on, the music started playing and I slowly started as if in a trance, the spotlight was on me and it soon changed to different colours whenever my moves changed from dynamic to soft or still as the music indicated. In the meantime, the rest of the room was in darkness, I could only see a few outlines of the audience.

I love dancing from the inside, but am aware I need to have contact with the audience so as to connect. I made sure I moved towards the front at times and used my long flowing arms to bring their attention to me. There was silence in the audience and I didn't know what they were thinking of my dancing, but I was hoping they could connect to the story that was moving through me.

It seemed liked the music went longer than I expected. I was lost in time. After what seemed so long it came to an end. The song finished and I came to a close and then the crowd started applauding loudly. I was grateful for this response and paused momentarily to acknowledge them.

I started walking off the stage area, when a couple of ladies ran towards me asking where I teach this dancing saying it was so sensual and fluid, a true Goddess dance! I was quite surprised that I had a couple of admirers, I thanked them, told them however I'm not doing anything at the moment, but would inform them if I opened up a studio in the near future. I watched the next few performances then went home that night, satisfied that I did it!

The next day someone from the audience contacted me on Facebook about posting a video of the dance I did. She had filmed it on her phone and wanted me to have a copy of it and get my permission to send it to me. I thought that was so nice of someone to do that for me as it is something I will keep forever as a memento of that night.

Dakini Dance – My Performance

This is how I feel when I dance ... a Dancing Dakini. I feel I am a Goddess through dance and my dancing is what has taken me through all my adventures in life.

28

Leo in Barcelona

Fast forward to the spring of 2017, and I travelled with my friend Jenny to Dubai and India. It was her first trip to Dubai, and the first time either of us had been to India.

It was quite an adventure travelling together, but our time in India was full of challenges. By the end, the constant haggling when buying goods became annoying. Once they saw you were a Westerner, they hiked up the prices. Some shops had a fixed price and then it was great knowing everyone had to pay the ticketed price, whether you were a local or a visitor.

We visited the Taj Mahal, explored a few different cities, shopped, and stayed in an ashram for a few days.

Once we got back to Dubai, Jenny left to go home for work while I stayed for a few more days.

I added Barcelona to my itinerary as I wanted to visit my friend Leo, whom I'd met in Melbourne through the Couch Surfing site.

Leo had contacted me to ask me to host him. In the past, I'd had a few negative experiences with men who rolled up in the late evening at my door, with strange energies and even bad body odour. So, anyone wanting to stay for free needed to meet me first – I would then decide if I could have them in my place.

I sent him a message to meet for a coffee and chat in Carlton, and he agreed. I drove to meet him at Brunetti café, and on entering a beautiful smile beamed at me – Leo!

We sat down and chatted. We got on so well, I immediately let him know he could stay. However, he had taken up another offer from a woman, so he had somewhere to stay. He just came to meet me. I told him about what I had been through with my cancer challenge and how it led me to change my diet and lifestyle.

He told me about his interest in spirituality, that he designed houses for community projects, travelled quite a bit and was originally from South America but grew up in Denmark.

He suggested we go for a walk to a nearby park. On the walk there, I had an incredible out-of-body experience. His presence triggered something within me, and I felt like I was walking on a cloud. My timing was in sync with him. Every step I took became more surreal – I felt a oneness of the universe. This went on for the duration of the short walk, and in that time, I don't recall a word being spoken between us. We seemed so connected that our presence was all that was needed.

We parted ways as soon as we arrived back at the meeting point. Leo smiled and said that he would keep in contact.

He lived up to his word and was soon sending me many emails, especially about health and spirituality. I was happy to receive them, and I mentioned that I would visit him one day. That's why I decided to go to see him in Barcelona. He had previously invited me to join him in Northern Italy where he was training in spirituality at a retreat called Damanhur.

Once I landed in Barcelona, I followed Leo's instructions and caught a local bus from the airport. It dropped me off at a major landmark close to his home.

I eventually found his home by asking the locals, who pointed the way. At the door, I was greeted by a tall, handsome guy who called out to Leo. Leo appeared looking strong, tanned, fit, and butt-naked.

I was taken aback, but he smiled, asked me in, and told me my room was made up. He even hinted that I could join him in his room if I ever wanted a cuddle. He said it was normal to see naked bodies around the house in the mornings.

After chatting for a little while, I entered my room. I felt exhausted, so decided to go to bed. Leo brought me a warm doona when I mentioned I was feeling cold.

I slept from the afternoon till the next morning – I was shivering at night and soon knew I was ill. I went to the kitchen in the morning to get some water and asked Leo if he had lemons so I could make up some warm water with lemon. He produced a bottle of Propolis – a natural antibiotic. It was a product I always turned to when I was sick, after using it during my first period of cancer symptoms.

I found out the markets were nearby, so I dragged myself out to buy more lemons, ginger, and Manuka honey. I bought a few healthy grocery items for the fridge and then came straight back to his house to sleep again.

For days, I was very ill. Leo cooked healthy casseroles and left me food to eat – he knew that I was unwell and couldn't do much.

His friend in the film industry was staying with him for a few days and had a bad cough, so I started making him up the same drink I was having with lemon, etc. By the end of his stay, he had totally recovered. He came and thanked me for caring so much, since I was in bed most of the day.

Leo was very hospitable and caring. After about four days in bed, I started feeling a bit stronger and was able to go out a few hours a day, mainly to buy food or look at clothes. Then I would go back to bed to rest or sleep.

In gratitude for his help, I took him out for dinner within walking distance and bought some food and wine, too. He was very generous to allow me to stay for 10 days.

I didn't feel the same with him as I had during our first encounter, and I thought being ill wouldn't have helped, either. He asked if I remembered the day we met. I thought he hadn't seen what had happened, but now I know he witnessed the shift and kept in contact after because of this.

The ten days were up and I had to leave the house – they were expecting friends to come stay in my room. I searched and found a woman, Patricia, nearby who had a bedroom available on the Homestay site. She offered me a discount and I booked in to stay.

I had packed lightly coming from Dubai, so I didn't have much to carry – and it turned out Patricia's house was only a few streets away!

Patricia was a local living with her young daughter, who went to stay with her dad while I was in her room. I got on well with the lady and she asked if I wanted to go out dancing one night. A night out in Barcelona!

I went out the next day to a nearby square called the Arc de Triomf – similar to the one in Paris. There was food, and locals were selling handmade goods. I found a small, precious bottle of Propolis, which I immediately bought – it had an amazing taste.

I heard live music, walked towards it and saw a guy dressed up like Michael Jackson, dancing away. He was great at impersonating Michael and even did the moon walk. I enjoyed watching him dance amongst hundreds of people – I wished I could do a dance myself.

He stopped after a few more songs and started playing recorded music loudly. The song was one of my favourites – 'Fresh' by Kool and the Gang.

I started moving in my space and gradually the music flowed through me. I couldn't stop – the beats and rhythm took over and I danced freely. People around me smiled back at me. The performer approached to see what was going on. He walked away scratching his head and came back with another dancer, who attempted to draw attention with his dancing.

The song finished and I thought to myself, I wish he would play it again. And he did! This time I really got into the song and danced energetically. Soon, I was getting the thumbs-up from people watching, and they were videoing me dance. I felt happy to dance again and liked that I was acknowledged, too. Dancing is my passion! I love seeing people enjoying themselves and being happy too!

I knew that I was healing now, as my energy had come back. I walked back to the new place I was staying at, went to my room, and slept soundly.

The next day I explored the festival site again, bought food, and met a man selling printed cotton spreads. The spreads were mainly for tourists wanting to sit on the grass area in Ciutadella Park. I ended up visiting him over my last few days, enjoying the afternoon sun and listening to buskers play nearby.

On the last night of my stay with the lady, we discussed going out to dance nearby that night. I was excited to finally have a good dance. We prepared ourselves and even had something to relax us before going out, thanks to a friend who dropped by.

We arrived at the club somewhat early and hung out in an area with a bar and few patrons. It was really quiet, and I wondered if it was worth coming. The music in the next room was slow and soft. Techno came on later, and I wasn't moved by it. However, I did want to dance, so I eventually just got up to dance and, sure enough, the music started improving and a few more people started dancing, too.

I was quite relaxed and into the flow. I wanted to explore more of the dance floor, so I started doing my signature pirouette moves. My new friend joined in, and eventually more and more people appeared out of nowhere to dance.

The dance floor was soon packed, and a group of young men danced close by. Later in the night, I got up to dance on a raised platform and they all imitated my moves. I was quite amused. One of them wanted a selfie with me and then rang his mother to tell her where he was. He said his mother was always telling him to be careful out at night and he wanted to tell her that she shouldn't worry – a woman her age was out dancing and outdoing everyone else.

He hung around for a while, but soon left with his friends. They all waved to me on their way out.

That night was absolutely amazing. A few guys came over to dance or asked me to join them. My friend was mainly chatting to a man, who in the end was quite abusive towards her.

I met a few older people who had dropped by and one gentleman went and brought water to me where I was dancing up on the platform. We started chatting, and he asked to meet up one day very soon.

I told him it was my last night – the next day I could meet him for a coffee near my place before I left for the airport.

We soon left the club, as the lady I went with was getting into an argument with a man, and it was not looking safe for her. I think she was too inebriated, and it was time to go.

The next day I met up with the gentleman and had a coffee nearby – which, I must say, was one of the worst coffees I've ever had. He was from another part of town and rode in on his scooter to meet me. He spoke about his business; they supplied ice-cream to many of the shops in Barcelona and said that we should keep in touch. I kept him on my Facebook contacts but deleted him later, as I thought I would never go back to Barcelona.

I went back to Dubai for a few more days after and collected my suitcase from a friend who had stored it, before finally heading home.

I noticed that I had a cyst-like growth under my left armpit. It was pulsating at times and got my attention.

Once I arrived back in Melbourne, I booked in to do some minor breast reconstruction and asked them to remove the growth there. It turned out to be a tumour and the nurse from the hospital rang me to say I needed chemo and radiotherapy, which I refused. I instead chose to eat well and not go down that route.

I went back to my part-time work as an extra in film or TV via the agency Real People, which I thoroughly enjoyed.

I thought nothing more about the tumour after it was removed. I just made sure I kept eating well, thinking right, and moving.

A few years later, I had the battle of my life.

29

COVID and Beyond

During the Covid pandemic, I felt there was so much evil unleashed onto the world. The lockdowns, the mental anguish, the constant media hype. Especially for us here in Melbourne, which was the most the locked-down city in the world. My stress levels were highly raised and I started searching the internet, listening to international speakers and felt that I wanted to pray more for humanity. I felt that I needed to meditate for the world because there was so much going on and it didn't sit right with me.

One night, I was staying at my girlfriend Jenny's house in a room she had rented out to a male friend who was away that weekend. I was lying in bed when I looked up to see a black mass of cloud-like appearance circling around. It was confined above my head and it looked menacing as it started to swirl towards my body and attempt to wrap itself around me. I automatically visualised a protective light around me to keep me safe. I had heard stories about Black Goo but wasn't absolutely sure what it was. It lingered around for a few minutes more then slowly disappeared. There were a couple more experiences around this time that jolted me to the point where I knew something wasn't right.

The stress of what was going on around me triggered my cancer to return and spread to other areas. This started with an infection in my back teeth. Eventually it progressed into my back being extremely painful. Around that time my mother was also experiencing a lot of back pain, more severe than anything she had before. She was taking lots of painkillers and was struggling with daily living. I wasn't able to help my mother because I was in a frail state myself. I was dependant on my sister to care for me, but I wanted her to stay with my mother because she also needed care – but my mother wouldn't allow her to leave my side.

When my mother was placed in palliative care, a nurse had seen me walking to her room and she looked at me in shock because I had lost so much weight and asked me if I needed a wheel chair. I didn't think I needed a wheelchair. My sisters and brothers were supposed to be there when I went to visit with my daughter, who had flown in from the Gold Coast. My siblings were late so I had time with her to do some healing and my mother was in a peaceful sleep. I felt that the healing helped her body and Soul. I visualised healing and wanted her Soul to pass onto a safe journey onto her next rebirth without so much suffering and in peace.

My sisters turned up an hour later saying they got on the wrong train and my brother said something had happened to his car and didn't turn up at all. I felt it was meant to be because I was able to do the healing without my siblings being there, because they wouldn't have given me the space to do this otherwise.

After her passing, my health deteriorated to the point of almost dying myself. I was crying virtually every day. I had two big tumours, pain in my lower back, no energy whatsoever. I had never experienced having no energy at all. I felt I like I was truly dying. I started using my Bioptron lamp to assist in my healing.

I used it day and night. No matter how exhausted I was, I kept putting the lamp on myself. The senior head oncologist didn't blink an eye when he saw the state I was in and placed me in palliative care at home. I chose to stay at home as I wanted to fight for my life with my healing tools close by. I visualised a lot throughout this time, meditated through my mind as I couldn't say the mantras out loud because my voice was so weak.

I then decided to move my body more. I had been on my back for at least six months without any movement, only to struggle to go the toilet and wash my body with a bowl of warm water and cloth, which my sister would prepare. I started exercising gently and placing my bed closer to the open bedroom window during the winter months that had some warmer days. The sunshine seemed to help my recovery and I was doing this as much as possible. My sister started preparing healthier meals through my direction and I had some friends come to do some juicing for me. The nurses that dropped in were astonished by my refusal to give in and even how I held on to the banister to walk down a flight of stairs in my state. When I couldn't get up from my couch I would push myself up with the help of my walking stick.

I went to do IV with vitamin C infusions regularly and had oxygen therapy, homeopathic appointments, infrared sauna and acupuncture. I was also having EE sessions, then having detox baths with salts after getting home. I think with all the toxins that came out, they triggered a seizure after I got out of the bath. The right side of my face and my arm were paralyzed. An ambulance was called but by the time they arrived the seizures were subsiding. I was taken to hospital for further testing and given medications but i chose not to take them once home after an over night stay there. I had one more seizure a few weeks later, but luckily I kept the bottle of blue liquid called Clonazepam.

My sister put it under my tongue and it subsided rather quickly. I ended up going to the NIIM Centre as I wasn't improving much. I booked to see the professor there, who was of enormous help. I was taken there now in a wheelchair, frail and sickly. He spent hours taking in my history, and prescribed me CBD oil and mentioned my seizures could have been triggered because of the tumors in my body. He also suggested I take Tomixfen tablets and I agreed reluctantly but took smaller doses, because my tumour was so large under my left armpit and I needed to shrink it. I was continuously going out in my frail state. My girlfriend Palma mentioned that people who are sick don't usually leave the house. Here I was, thanks to a male friend called John, who drove me around to my appointments and to the local shops. I was still trying to move independently without my walking stick by holding onto anything within my reach to support myself.

There was an incident where I used to go to a café frequently and the coffee maker avoided eye contact with me because of the state I was in. I was down to forty-seven kilos from seventy-five. My girlfriend Sue mentioned that she would miss me when I go whilst shedding tears. Everyone was expecting me to die. With the encouragement of my daughter and help from my son who got my story off my old computer, it inspired me to get my story out into the world to help others.

Today in 2024, I have put on over ten kilos and people have commented on my improvement. My energies are moving around my lung and chest area, it's light and breezy, pulsating at times. This is something new and I have never felt this before, but I know this is healing me.

I felt this new challenge cemented my inner power to shine through. My mind has sharpened, and my warrior aspect has surfaced. I feel more determined now, and know that we are more powerful than we believe. The power is within us, not outside.

Everything outside of us is a distraction from who we really are. We need to look inside ourselves and explore our inner deep core to find our truth. Doing this will result in peace and inner happiness.

I have faced death and fought to be here. I didn't want others to decide for me. With this new inner strength in writing this book, I'm hoping my health will continue to improve and I can keep dancing through to the light.

See you on the dance floor.

Acknowledgements and Reflections

You learn from every person that enters your life, we are both students and teachers. There are some people that just don't resonate at my level – people that I've attracted into my life – I believe to show me that I need to work more on myself. I've met people that I thought were going to become friends and the next day they are gone. I understand now that they only came to me as messengers, to tell me something I needed to hear.

I was seeking to find happiness outside of me in my early youth and adult years. Buddhism helped me start looking within, although I did go off the track many times. I always came back to who I am, a Soul first.

Whilst I was questioning why I had to go through so much suffering, I asked for guidance through my meditation. I have been meditating for over forty years now and this has helped tame the thoughts in my head from the self-abuse I inflicted to myself through not loving myself. It's taken me a very long time to heal. Meditating, I know, has helped me still be here today.

When I was told I needed to start treatments for the cancer and I was going out of my mind about whether to have the chemotherapy, radiotherapy and tablets. I had so many different opinions and even a letter from a man who lost his wife to cancer because she didn't do the treatments. I was so confused and one evening I listened to Bashar and the talk really resonated with me fully and that was when I decided not to go down that path. I am indebted to Spirit for guiding me there to seek for answers. I am so at peace with that decision.

Throughout it all, I have to say that my dancing has been there for my healing, assisting me through all the pain and suffering. Every time after surgery when I was well enough, I would go dancing with my friend Judy and dance my pain away. To get back into my light was the most healing through dance.

I also practice gratitude as much as needed. I thank God for many things. I bless my bed for being so comfortable and for many lovely surprises that come into my life. It's always nice to give a compliment when needed and from the heart. It's very uplifting and can make a difference to a person's day or even life.

I am grateful for having two beautiful grown-up children Adele and Calvin, who I have learnt so much from and love dearly. My mother who had always been there for me, the kindest woman on Earth to me. She had always been there for me for all my needs and emotional support. My sisters and brothers, we have always stuck together as a family. My Dad who has passed just over nine years ago, I miss him, even though he was tough. I saw the softness in his heart open at the end.

I thank all who entered my life as friends, whether short or long.

Acknowledgements and Reflections

**Always listen to your intuition
and follow your passion.**

*The answer is to
give and receive*
LOVE

www.ingramcontent.com/pod-product-compliance
Lightning Source LLC
Chambersburg PA
CBHW030037100526
44590CB00011B/240